by Louis MacNeice

a play in two acts

OUT OF
THE PICTURE

Faber and Faber Limited
24 Russell Square
London

First published in June Mcmxxxvii
By Faber and Faber Limited
24 Russell Square London W.C. 1
Second impression October Mcmxxxvii
Printed in Great Britain by
R. MacLehose and Company Limited
The University Press Glasgow

To

GRAHAM and ANNE SHEPARD

This play is to be produced during the summer of
1937 by the Group Theatre and Rupert Doone with
music by Benjamin Britten and sets and costumes by
Robert Medley.

CAST

Portright
Miss Haskey
Two framer's men
Bailiff
Moll O'Hara
Dr. Spielmann
Clara de Groot
Mrs. Freudenberg
Auctioneer
Collectors
Sir Sholto Spielmann
Sir Sholto's Secretary
Venus
Listener-In, Radio-Announcer, etc.

ACT I

ACT I

SCENE I

[PORTRIGHT'S *room in a basement, empty.* RADIO
SET, *telephone.*]

RADIO SET [*suddenly*]. Special Morning News Bulletin: Geneva. The Peace Conference will resume its
session today to discuss any last-minute measures
possible to prevent the outbreak of war. Experts
consider that the prospects of a satisfactory solution being found to the present economic and political deadlock are, if not insurmountable, at least—

PORTRIGHT [*entering and hurriedly turning it off*].
These mechanical appliances! They like the sound
of their own voice. [*Telephone rings.*] There you are,
you see, there you are. [*Takes up receiver.*] Hullo!
Hullo! Good morning, Mr. Eli! She's coming? Oh
splendid! Splendid, Mr. Eli, marvellous! I wasn't
expecting her so soon. What? Straight away? Marvellous, Mr. Eli. I'll expect her in five minutes'
time. [*Rings off.*] [*Theatrically.*] 'She is coming, my
own, my sweet—'

[*Enter* MISS HASKEY.]

9

Miss H. Have you eaten your breakfast yet?

Portright. I'm waiting for the coffee.

Miss H. Then you're waiting for the Millennium.

Portright. Eh? What do you mean?

Miss H. You won't get any coffee.

Portright. Why not?

Miss H. Why not, he asks, why not! I'll tell you for the tenth time. You can't have any coffee because there's no way of boiling the coffee. The gas company have cut off the gas. [*After a pause.*] I suppose you want to know *why* they've cut off the gas.

Portright. Yes, Why have they cut off the gas?

Miss H. Because you never pay the gas bill.

Portright. Don't I? I paid it once, I think.

Miss H. Oh what would your poor father say! It was thirty years ago I went to live at the Hall—you were only a toddler then—and never did I think— debts, oh dear—never did I think that your father's only son—of course I didn't know your poor father was going to lose all his money and your dear mother not being quite right after that but all the same a gentleman ought to pay his debts. I shall have to get you a new spike to put the bills on.

Portright. Miss Haskey, I am an artist. I must have something to drink with my breakfast.

Miss H. Milk then, milk! There it is in the cracked cup.

Portright. Milk! Well, I suppose I shall have to come to it. Facilis descensus Averno, you know. One gets tuberculosis from drinking milk. [*Takes a*

10

sip.] It has a very unpleasant taste. [*Suddenly.*]
Miss Haskey, I have an inspiration. When you say
we cannot have coffee, you mean that we cannot
boil the water for the coffee. Presumably the coffee
itself—the powder you know—we have plenty of
that?

MISS H. We have a little ground coffee which I bought
out of my savings.

PORTRIGHT. Then everything's all right. Take your
ground coffee and cook it in the electric kettle.

MISS H. Really, Mr. Portright! I sometimes wonder—

PORTRIGHT. What's wrong now?

MISS H. I've told you a dozen times if I've told you
once. The electric company have cut off the electricity.

PORTRIGHT. Oh.

MISS H. [*beginning to cry*]. Why don't you try to make
some money, Mr. Portright.

[*The doorbell rings upstairs.*]

PORTRIGHT. Ah, who do you think that is?

MISS H. The bailiff I dare say.

PORTRIGHT. Wrong, Miss Haskey. It's not a he, it's a
she.

MISS H. What! I've told you you can't have lady visi-
tors here.

[*Bell rings again.*]

PORTRIGHT. You'd better answer it, Miss Haskey.
[MISS H. *goes out and can be heard mounting the
stairs.*]

PORTRIGHT. What is gas? What is electricity? What,

11

for that matter, is coffee? Other people sit over their replenished breakfast-tables but by comparison with me—by comparison with me—This is my lucky day, gentlemen,

> She is coming, my own, my sweet,
> With ever so airy a tread—There she is now!

[*Heavy steps are heard descending the stairs. A crash against the door.*]

Come in, darling, come in.

[*Two workmen enter with a crate.*]

1ST MAN. Here she is, Mister.

2ND MAN. We haven't half had a job with her on these here stairs of yours.

1ST MAN. No. They don't build houses this way now.

PORTRIGHT. My beloved! Our painful separation is over. I trust you came to no harm with Mr. Eli.

2ND MAN. That she didn't! Mr. Eli's made a picture of her.

PORTRIGHT. Good God, what do you mean? Made a picture of her? But my good man, she *is* a picture.

2ND MAN. Oh I know she's a picture but I mean he's made a picture of her. You wait till you see the frame he's put on her.

PORTRIGHT. And not too much varnish, I hope? That's right, men, open her up. But go careful for God's sake, go careful.

1ST MAN. That's all right, Mister. We'll treat her like she was a bagful of eggs.

2ND MAN. Eggs is one-and-eleven these days. I was carryin' some home for the Missus and God Almighty

12

if I didn't go and walk on a banana. Oh, she gave me a towelling, I can tell you.

1ST MAN. Here, you get up on top of her, Bill. You always was a one for heights.

2ND MAN. Here goes. High as a stinking fish I am now. Is this ceiling safe, guvnor, or what happens if I put my head through it?

1ST MAN. Prise her now, Bill, prise her.

2ND MAN. Ah, here she comes. All together.

PORTRIGHT. What bliss! She has been away ten days. But she has never been here before. Always in the studio. She ought to like it here, I think. I've made this little place quite comfortable.

[*As the picture is being lifted out of the crate,* MISS HASKEY *enters.*]

MISS H. What is that?

PORTRIGHT. That is my masterpiece.

MISS H. You mean you painted that?

PORTRIGHT. Of course I painted it.

MISS H. [*slightly impressed*]. Well, I never heard of you painting a picture before.

PORTRIGHT. Miss Haskey, you have such a sense of humour. Don't you know I'm a painter?

MISS H. Oh I know you're a *painter*!

PORTRIGHT. Now I know exactly what you're thinking. I quite admit I don't usually finish my pictures. That's because I have such a conscience. As a matter of fact this is the first painting I have ever completed quite completely. That is why I have had a real gilt frame made for it by Eli's.

13

Miss H. Who's going to pay for the frame?

Portright. No one, I should think. [*Agitation among the men.*] No, no, don't mind what I said. That was just a joke. Don't repeat it to Mr. Eli. Just a joke, you know, just a joke.

Miss H. Let me put on my glasses. Now then. Let us have a look at it.

Portright. She is called the Rising Venus.

Miss H. [*after a pause*]. Oh, *is* she? She looks to me a good deal more like that Miss O'Hara.

Portright. Who is Miss O'Hara?

Miss H. Now don't you come that over me. I thought I asked you not to employ any models without consulting me.

Portright. But, Miss Haskey, I never employ any models.

Miss H. Yes, you did. That's Miss O'Hara. Moll O'Hara they call her. And if you had to pick a model—what would your poor mother say? Those poor Italian girls who don't know any better, that's one thing. And I *am* told they do their best to behave themselves though it must be very hard behaving without any clothes. But Miss O'Hara hasn't got their excuse because her father was a general and anyway, she enjoys it. She's an immoral woman.

2nd Man. Hear, hear; that's what *I* say.

Portright. Miss Haskey, you must believe me. If my picture looks like Miss O'Hara, it must be a pure coincidence. [*The bell rings above.*]

14

MISS H. There's that bell again. Nothing but trouble this morning. [*Goes out.*]

2ND MAN. A bit squally, that one.

MISS H. [*from above*]. Mr. Portright, you're wanted upstairs.

[PORTRIGHT *goes out.*]

1ST MAN. Crazy layout this. The old girl don't let him have models. But it's Miss O'Hara all right. I've seen her dozens of times. Eli's fair sick of her.

2ND MAN. You're wrong. That ain't Moll. Leastways it ain't a good resemblance. Besides, what would she be doing in the sea? Sofas now . . . I'll bet you half-a-crown that ain't Moll.

1ST MAN. I take you, Bill.

2ND MAN. I mean, just look at them white horses.

[*Noise of descending steps and voices in argument. Enter* PORTRIGHT, MISS HASKEY *and* BAILIFF.]

BAILIFF [*standing in middle of stage and declaiming*].

I have come to enforce the laws of property

I, the bailiff, the embodiment of civilisation.

Whoso walks in the ways of solvency

Whoso cherishes and practises the social contract

Whoso pays his debts with integrity and punctuality,

On him I lay no hand,

He enjoys my respect and the absence of my person.

But those who are asocial, immoral, parasitic, anarchic.

15

Those who think that they are a law to themselves—

Good God! There's Miss O'Hara.

1st Man. My half-crown, please.

2nd Man. No, it ain't proved yet. How would *he*
know?

Miss H. Mr. Portright, I am deeply ashamed.

Portright. Are you? What are you ashamed of?

Miss H. Of you, Mr. Portright, you, your father's son.
It was bad enough to have used Miss O'Hara for a
model. But to have told an untruth to one who
always—

Portright. Now Miss Haskey, let me explain.

Bailiff. Come, come, sir. We've got to get a move
on. I have my orders to distrain on all this
property.

Portright. Just one moment, please. Listen to me,
Miss Haskey. I am an artist who has no need of
models. I have it all in here. [*Taps his forehead.*]
The true artist has his eye not on a particular person but on a transcendent model which exists in
the world not of Becoming but of Being. Miss
O'Hara and all the other models of your ordinary
hand-to-mouth painters belong in the world of
Becoming. This picture was painted from the im-
mortal pattern, the Platonic Idea.

2nd Man. Platonic Idea! I told you so. Those ain't
Miss O'Hara's legs.

Portright. Why should we always work at a remove
from reality? Miss O'Hara, whoever she is, is

16

merely herself a copy. She is in no sense an original. If I imitate her form in a painting, I merely reproduce her own deviations from truth.

MISS H. I'm sure she has plenty of them.

PORTRIGHT. The Rising Venus is a primal and an ultimate conception. If you have ever read Lucretius—

BAILIFF. Look here, sir, I'm here to do my duty and I'm going to do it. All this property's got to go. *And* that picture along with it. [*The bell rings above.*]

PORTRIGHT. What!

MISS H. There's something in a bailiff after all.

BAILIFF. Look here, men, lend me a hand will you? My own men have gone off to enlist. They think there's going to be a war or something.

1ST MAN. Well, even so, what do they want to enlist for?

BAILIFF. So as to be safer from the air-raids. [*Steps on the stairs.*]

2ND MAN. Who'll this be, I wonder.

PORTRIGHT. You can't take my picture, you can't take it, you can't!

[*Enter* MOLL O'HARA.]

MISS H. Who are you? Well, if it isn't—

MOLL. My name's O'Hara. Where's Portright?

MISS H. So you'd never heard of her?

1ST MAN. 'And over that 'arf-crown.

MOLL. Portright!

PORTRIGHT. Oh hullo, yes, hullo.

MOLL. Portright, I've come to dun you.

1ST MAN. Another of 'em!

PORTRIGHT. How much do you want?

MOLL. My fee. Ten guineas.

PORTRIGHT. Oh, ten guineas?

MOLL. You know that already. What's going on here?

PORTRIGHT. Oh this is nothing. Just some friends dropped in.

MISS H. It's the bailiffs.

MOLL. Oh. Well, bailiffs or not, I want ten guineas.

MISS H. Mr Portright, I feel compelled to give you my notice.

PORTRIGHT. What, Miss Haskey? Oh, certainly.

MISS H. You accept it!

PORTRIGHT. I would accept anything in these circumstances.

MISS H. He accepts my notice! [*She goes out crying.*]

PORTRIGHT. Miss O'Hara, you must listen to me. I am a man of few words. This scourge of God, what they call a bailiff, is carrying away all my belongings. That I do not so much mind. But my picture, the Rising Venus, the only picture which I have ever completed—

MOLL. Rising Venus! You got a rise out of me, didn't you? Well, a bad debt, I suppose. Good morning all.

PORTRIGHT. No, no, don't go, Miss O'Hara. I should like to talk to you, you have a kind face. Everyone is leaving me. Miss Haskey has already gone who was thirty years with the family. And now my Venus. [*Gulps with emotion.*] Look, Miss O'Hara, have some milk. [*Offers her the cup.*]

18

BAILIFF. Here, you can't drink that!

MOLL. Can't I? [*Drinks.*]

BAILIFF. Well, I'll trouble you for the cup.

MOLL. There you are, dearie. He likes his pound of flesh, that man.

PORTRIGHT [*reflectively*]. Yes, he is like Genghiz Khan. He leaves a desolation behind him. [*The picture is now carried out after the other furniture.*]

PORTRIGHT [*dropping on his knees and blowing kisses*]. Good-bye, darling, good-bye.

> [*The door closes on the* BAILIFF, *the* TWO MEN *and the picture. They are heard crashing up the stairs.*]

Oh infamy! Oh mutilation!

MOLL. I suppose you thought I gave you all those sittings for love?

PORTRIGHT. Love?

MOLL. Love, alias gratis.

PORTRIGHT. Oh no, I really meant to pay you. I didn't know a bailiff was going to come.

MOLL. Ten guineas! Well, well, it's lucky some of you painters pay. You're hardly a painter though, of course.

PORTRIGHT. What!

MOLL. Now don't be cross. I mean you're more what one would call an amateur.

PORTRIGHT. This is the last insult! Where is the gas oven? [*Rushes dramatically to the gas cooker, turns on the tap and listens.*] What is this? There is no gas! Frustration, frustration everywhere! Very well

19

then, as I cannot commit suicide, perhaps you will apologise to me?

MOLL. Perhaps *I* will apologise to *you*!

PORTRIGHT. For calling me—I can't say it, I can't say it.

MOLL. An amateur, you mean? Now look here, Portright. I know something about painting—I've been painted more than any other woman in London—and I can tell you this. That picture of yours (for which you condescended to use me as a model gratis in your exceedingly draughty and evil-smelling studio), that fancy picture of yours is nothing but a rotten pastiche. To start with, it is a travesty of Botticelli.

PORTRIGHT. Ah, but it is meant to be. It is Botticelli with a difference.

MOLL. Yes, I see that. And I don't mind so much what you've done to Botticelli but look what you've done to me. First of all you've put me in the uncomfortable position of the Botticelli Venus. Then, in order to be a little modern, you've twisted and elongated my neck à la Modigliani (he's out of date now and he was a bad painter anyway), then you've done away with my legs and put someone else's in their place though whose they can be I can't imagine. As for the total result I admit that it's pretty in the worst manner possible but it isn't even any use as sex-appeal. It's frigid. Look at me. If you wanted to paint somebody frigid, why didn't you try Clara de Groot?

PORTRIGHT. You mean the film star?

MOLL. Well, I hope there's no one else with such a damn silly name.

PORTRIGHT. But Clara de Groot? She wouldn't have sat for me.

MOLL. Maybe not, but you can see her picture on every hoarding in this town. All you've got to do is copy one of those, put in a bit of Modigliani—

PORTRIGHT. Clara de Groot *is* very beautiful of course.

MOLL. You *would* think so! You're like all the others.

PORTRIGHT. But you don't understand that I didn't really want a model.

MOLL. What!

PORTRIGHT. I mean the model was merely incidental.

MOLL. Really, I wish I'd known that before.

PORTRIGHT. What I was trying to express was not any particular human beauty, but the principle of love itself—

MOLL. Now don't go over all that. I had enough of that in the studio.

PORTRIGHT. Love, Miss O'Hara, love is the only thing left to us.

MOLL. You don't say!

PORTRIGHT. Yes. I am an individualist.

MOLL. That's one name for it. But I'm afraid your bailiff has taken away the bed.

PORTRIGHT. The bed?

MOLL. Never mind. [*Suddenly becoming serious.*] Look, Portright, I'm sorry for you. Because you're mad. You're either mad or ill. What do you want out of life at all? Don't you want to make some money?

PORTRIGHT. No. I want to create.

MOLL. Create what?

PORTRIGHT. Just create. [*A long pause.*]

Perhaps I am ill. Perhaps I am mad. I know what you want. You want to set the psychologists on me to dig me to pieces with scalpels. Or you want to set the communists on me to make me a cog in a gearbox. Or you want to set the stormtroopers on me to make a man of me with truncheons. Don't you now, don't you?

MOLL. No, my dear, I don't.

PORTRIGHT. Oh I can see through you all right. To hell with you I say. To hell with everyone who is successful and interfering—

MOLL. Am I successful and interfering?

PORTRIGHT. I am here in my corner and here I stay. Do you think *I'm* going to get mixed up in any world movements? Going on a rotten crusade that's timed by Bradshaw? No, I'm not. Anyone else may but not me. I'm glad I am where I am and to be what I am—

I exult in neuroses, psychoses, the delight of defeat,

The aura of failure, the strength of anaemia,

The haunted sleep of the emphatically lost,

The parade of golden ghosts in the drugged mind.

None of you can take this from me

None of you strong men, community tyrants,

With your hammers and sickles and pudding
    moulds

And nibs that scratch on parchment graphs and
    charts.

I have still myself even if I have lost my picture.

MOLL [*clapping*]. You're coming on, my dear, you
speak very nicely. And have you forgotten all about
that picture now?

PORTRIGHT. I shall never forget her.

MOLL. Her? You mean *it*.

PORTRIGHT. I mean her.

MOLL [*whistles*]. So that's it.

PORTRIGHT. That's what?

MOLL. Nothing. Wasn't there someone called Pyg-
malion once?

PORTRIGHT. Just a moment. Just a moment. I have
more to say. [*Begins to declaim.*]

They have taken her from me, my picture,

The apple of my eye, the pulse of my heart,

That butcher the bailiff and his meddling minions

Who have no respect for an artist.

For I am an artist, I have an individual eye,

An original touch, a unique conception,

Like Michelangelo.

And I have spent a great deal of time and money
    in becoming one,

I studied at the Slade and under Choux-Crout
    in Paris,

Then I came home and rented a studio in Surbiton;

I have worked ten years and never finished a
    picture.
Why?
Because of my unique discrimination and self ab-
    negation.
I have scrapped them by bushels.
This is the first that I have finished.
I have taste, you see;
You will not know what that is, you are the
    crowd,
The crowd has no taste.
If you want to have taste you need to spend
    money and time
And mix with people who know and be born
    with a *je ne sais quoi*—
Like me in fact.
You would not know that it is right to prefer
    Giotto to Raphael,
The Apollo at Olympia to the Hermes of Praxi-
    teles,
Poussin to Titian, Manet to Monet, Paestum to
    the Parthenon,
Stein to Stone and Sung to Ming,
The Bison of the Stone Age to the rapportage of
    the Bushmen,
The bronzes of Benin to the Palace of Ver-
    sailles—
No, no, you could never possibly attain to it.
But think of the tragedy of it—
I have taste and you have not

24

But you are happy and I am not.

Here have I been aloof, alone from the mob,

Working under difficulties physical, spiritual and
financial,

Despised and ignored by those who are commer-
cially successful

(But what is commercial success?),

Suffering from bad light (they said it was north
but it isn't), no heating, a smell on the landing,

The desire for impossible perfection, asthma and
constipation,

Tradesmen's bills, landlady's anger, little boys'
laughter, critics' contempt—

All this I have put up with,

The great idea was forthcoming in my sub-
conscious

Slowly emerging to light, compact and crystal,

My Alter Ego, the work in which I found myself,

My pearl-oyster hidden in the depths, my ship-
wrecked statue, my lost key,

My Rising Venus, irresistibly rising out of the
daily sea.

MOLL. And where do I come in on that?

PORTRIGHT. You? You don't come in.

MOLL. Then I'll be going.

PORTRIGHT. No, no, don't go. I am lonely.

MOLL. The hell you are! [*A pause.*]

Portright. Would you like me to get you back
your picture?

25

PORTRIGHT. Yes. Can you?

MOLL. Of course I can.

PORTRIGHT. But *how* can you do that?

MOLL. Oh, just by taking action.
Ever heard of action?
It's something they do among the barbarians.
But there's a condition attached to it.

PORTRIGHT. To what?

MOLL. If I get this picture back for you, will you swear
to do something for me in return?

PORTRIGHT. What?

MOLL. That's a secret. Come on. Say after me:
If Moll O'Hara gets my picture back for me
I will do one thing for her in return,
Whatever she chooses to ask,
So help me God
If there is One. [*He repeats this after her.*]

MOLL. Good. I'm going now. Meet me outside Schat-
zen's Tourist Agency at three sharp this afternoon.
We may have to go to an auction?

PORTRIGHT. An auction?

MOLL. Lindenbaum's are holding an auction this afternoon. Your picture may possibly be there.

PORTRIGHT. Oh, Miss O'Hara, can I ever thank you
enough?

MOLL. Leave that for the moment. Well, see you at
three. Good-bye! [*She goes out.*]

PORTRIGHT. What a strange woman! A pity about the
ten guineas. I shall have to save up. [*Walks up and
down the empty basement.*] They might have left me

a chair, I think. Life is too hard, you know, too hard altogether.

[*Walks forward and sings or recites to the audience:*]

O had I the wings of an eagle or condor
Or a silver 'plane
I would leave tomorrow for Schlaraffenland or
     Fairyland
Nephelokokkūgia or the Land of Cockayne
Where tarts fall into the mouth
And roast pigs walk
And the full-blown body stuffs itself and feels no
     pain.

But stuck in a world of life-insurances
I cannot fly
I cannot attain the effulgence of self-indulgence
The ascetic's mystery or the artist's eye;
My hands, my lips, my loins
And my hungry guts
Will go unsatisfied until the day I die.

[*He begins to walk off but stops and says conversationally:*]

But all the same, you know, I wouldn't be anyone else.

CURTAIN

[*Before the* CURTAIN. LISTENER-IN, *L. Microphone, R.*]

LISTENER-IN [*looking at his watch*]. Just about time for the Lunch-Hour Talk. What are they having to-day, I wonder. [*Turns on radio.*]

RADIO-ANNOUNCER [*rushing up breathlessly to microphone begins to sing*]—

> 'Since when it grows, and smells, I swear,
> Not of itself but thee!'

> [*Taking three steps back and forward again; in his own voice*]—

You have just heard Mr. Tom Raglan singing 'Drink to Me Only'. This concludes our midday concert. I have now great pleasure in introducing to you Professor Joseph Vint who is going to give us a lunch-hour talk on the subject of—the subject of Aristotle and the Modern Stage. Professor Joseph Vint!

> [*Steps back and forward again, puts on a false moustache and pince-nez.*]

When Napoleon turned away from Moscow—but perhaps you are wondering why I begin in this way. What had Napoleon to do with Aristotle? Very

28

little. And what has Moscow to do with Aristotle? But before I answer that, I must remind you of a certain Russian writer whose plays a few years ago had a temporary vogue in London. I mean Anton Tchekov. Tchekov wrote a number of plays which were all the same and he had a number of heroes who were all the same. These heroes were without exception singularly unheroic. In that they were the antithesis of Napoleon. But they had one thing in common with Napoleon and that was that neither Napoleon nor they could ever get into Moscow— once they had turned their back on it. We know what this did to Napoleon but what did it do to the young men in Tchekov. To put it in the barest phraseology, it rotted them up. To be excluded for ever from that great city, the culture, the caviare, the interminable brilliant conversations—this was something which the young men could not face. So they started shooting. Such is the one and only plot of Tchekov. Now Aristotle wouldn't have liked that sort of plot. Aristotle insisted on unity and dignity. Further, Aristotle liked to know where he was. He liked to know whether he was in a tragedy or a comedy. But in these plays of Tchekov and many other plays which have succeeded them, who is to say? One moment you are laughing at the foibles of the characters and the next moment you find they have shot themselves. Terribly inconsequent; but, ladies and gentlemen, terribly true to life. That does not vindicate it, of course. Why

29

should one be true to life in a play? I don't know. You don't know. Most of us, I think, prefer a heroic falsification. If we have to retreat from Moscow we should wish to do it like Napoleon—

LISTENER-IN. What *is* all this about? [*Turns it off.*] Can one get anything decent at this hour? [*Tries another station.*]

RADIO-ANNOUNCER [*as before*]—which only bears out what Aristotle says in his famous chapter on catharsis—

LISTENER-IN. Oh damn. [*Tries another station.*]

RADIO-ANNOUNCER [*throwing away his pince-nez and moustache, begins to sing in nigger fashion*]—

> Oh in da moon
> Oh in da moon
> Oh in da moo-oo-oo-oo-oo.

[*The* LISTENER-IN *turns knob again. R.A. feverishly begins to look about on the floor for his pince-nez and false moustache. Silence.*]

LISTENER-IN. Well, what's wrong with the machine?

RADIO-ANNOUNCER [*rushing up to microphone, having found his appurtenances*]—so that I cannot myself see why the transition from comic to tragic, *or* back again, *or* backwards and forwards *or* round and round, which is after all only in accordance with the rules or lack of rules of ordinary existence, ordinary life as you can see from the daily press being in the nature of a game of snakes and ladders, I cannot therefore, see—

[*Stops short, gasps, removes pince-nez and mous-*

tache, puts them in his pocket and speaks as ANNOUNCER]—

The ordinary programme is being interrupted in order to give all listeners the latest information on the all-important Peace Conference which is being held today in Geneva. The Conference met at 9.30 sharp this morning. It was hoped till the last moment that those nations which have up to now abstained from taking part in this conference would at this eleventh hour of universal crisis send representatives—

LISTENER-IN. Oh, I can't bear this. [*Turns radio off.*] Always the same old story. Conferences! Conferences! Nothing decent now, I suppose, till the children's hour. I'll just run through the stations. [*He busily manipulates his radio set.* RADIO-ANNOUNCER *begins to beat a drum and various other performers enter, R.—a woman crooner, a clergyman, a cellist, etc. They begin to do their own turns regardless of each other.*]

Good Lord! How these stations all butt in on each other. Must be the weather, I think. Nothing to do but turn the damn thing off. [*He turns off the wireless and the performers march off.*]

31

ACT I

SCENE II

[Dr. Spielmann's *Consulting Room:* Spielmann *and* Clara de Groot. Bill the Parrot *in a Cage.*]

Clara. I had a dream about a green bird in green trees.

Spielmann. Now, my dear, if you don't mind just going through our usual little procedure and telling me everything that happened in your dream from the beginning, without addition and without subtraction, in the simplest possible language—

Clara. But, Dr. Spielmann, there was nothing else in the dream. Just a green bird in green trees.

Spielmann. Oh there must have been more than that. What about yourself in the dream? What were your reactions to the bird?

Clara. Oh I don't think I had any reactions. I remember one thing though. I was wearing a dress of peau d'éléphant.

Spielmann. A dress of what did you say?

Clara. Peau d'éléphant.

Bill [*bawls*]. Elephant skin.

Spielmann. Yes, of course, I didn't quite catch you.

32

Well then, you were wearing this dress when you saw the bird. What else about the bird? What did he do?

CLARA. I don't know, doctor.

SPIELMANN. Well, did he fly about or was he sitting still on a twig?

CLARA. I don't know, Dr. Spielmann. I couldn't see the bird. You see, he was a green bird in green trees.

SPIELMANN. Well, perhaps you could hear him? We must have some more details. A dream without details is useless. No doubt you heard him singing? What kind of a song would you say he had? Or perhaps you are not very well acquainted with the different woodnotes wild of our feathered—

CLARA. The bird was not singing.

SPIELMANN. Good. That is something established. The bird was not singing. A negative is a positive in psychology, you know. In fact it is just like photography. *You* take the photographs; *we* develop them. But let us continue. What other facts were there about the bird?

CLARA. That's everything, doctor. A green bird in green trees. Not singing. I couldn't see him. I couldn't hear him. I was wearing a dress of peau d'éléphant.

SPIELMANN. Excellent. A green bird in green trees and quite silent.

BILL. Looks bad, don't you think?

SPIELMANN. Silence, Bill! Well, my dear, this is a very interesting dream. I shall collate it with your other

C

dreams, of which I have the typed analyses in this file. The dream is, of course, a transparent one. Would you like me to interpret its symbolism?

CLARA. Oh yes, Dr. Spielmann. You're my oracle, **you** know.

SPIELMANN. The green bird is, of course, yourself.

CLARA. He couldn't be myself, doctor, because I was outside him. I was wearing a dress—

SPIELMANN. That makes no difference, my dear. In dreams, and for that matter in our waking existence, the self is often divided in that way. The green bird is yourself. The green trees represent your professional existence.

CLARA. Why?

SPIELMANN. Oh it is quite obvious, my dear. A bird lives in trees, an actress lives on the stage—

BILL. Or on the screen.

SPIELMANN. Or on the screen. If you represent the bird, I mean if the bird represents you, the trees must represent the stage.

BILL. Or the screen.

SPIELMANN. Quite right. Or the screen.

CLARA. It doesn't seem very convincing to me.

BILL. What about greenroom?

SPIELMANN. Greenroom?

BILL. Greenroom: green trees. Green trees: greenroom. Where the actors go when you don't see 'em.

SPIELMANN. That was a point I was going to make myself. Bill has lived with me so long that he has quite picked up the technique. Do you see now, my dear?

34

Greenroom is what we call the middle term. The green trees, therefore, as I have said, represent your professional existence. The point of the dream is that you are afraid your professional existence may usurp or obsess all of your other existences.

CLARA. I haven't got any other existences.

SPIELMANN. That is just my point. You are afraid, though the fear is strongly repressed in your hours of waking, that you will be lost in a world on one plane or of one colour—

CLARA. Lost! What do you mean by lost? Do you mean that I, I Clara de Groot, who stand out head and shoulders—

SPIELMANN. No, of course, I wouldn't dream of meaning that. You will always be at the head of your profession, my dear. On the contrary. The higher you ascend in your profession, the more likely you are to be cut off from the world of actual life, a world not of painted perspectives or cardboard sets, but of streets which lead to something, of trains with engines attached to them, of doors which open into houses, of men and women who live and die, make money and lose it, make love and bear children, not to the neat design of a theatrical producer but according to the vast chaotic untidy lack of design of Nature. Yet who knows if the apparent irrelevance, the inchoate status, of the non-artistic world is not itself a design of an infinitely wider pattern, too great for our weak eyes to apprehend, undefined merely because unexplored,

35

like Terra Incognita on ancient maps, who knows
if everything from the electrons in the kitchen table
to the flash of genius in an inventor's mind or the
navel-contemplation of the Hindu saint, saying Om
Om indefinitely, who knows if all these things,
spiritual or material as we crudely distinguish them,
are not merely movements in a vast ballet or opera
or notes in a score of music—

BILL. 'E's been reading them books of Popular
Physics.

CLARA. Dr. Spielmann, what are you doing? Are you
lecturing me?

SPIELMANN. We never lecture. We merely lead by the
hand.

CLARA. Then why can't you ever lead me somewhere
nice? You may not believe me but I'm really very
unhappy.

SPIELMANN. Naturally I believe you. It is an axiom. If
you were not unhappy, what would you be doing
here?

CLARA. Anyway, Dr. Spielmann, I've been coming to
you for weeks, absolutely weeks, and you haven't
even diagnosed me yet.

BILL. All pre-natal, that's what it is.

CLARA. Why do you keep that bird, doctor? He gets on
my nerves.

SPIELMANN. Would you like me to put him out?

CLARA. It's too late now. The harm's done. I shall have
a headache for the rest of the day.

SPIELMANN. Bill, how often have I told you—

BILL. Shut it. You'd be nowhere without me. Would he, ma'am?

SPIELMANN. Bill, if you say another word I'll put you out.

BILL. That's all right with me. I don't want to talk. I'm a listener, I am. Well, 'ere's your very good 'ealth and now I'm going to bye-bye. [*Begins to snore.*]

CLARA. Thank God! And now, doctor, please, please tell me what's the matter with me. Why should I feel as I do? My complexion is all right, my figure is just where I want it, my salary has never been bigger (no one's has, for that matter), and yet, doctor, and yet . . .

SPIELMANN. I'm sorry, my dear, but I can't tell you very much at present. People in my line of business need time. Only a quack will make a pronouncement during the first six months of consultations.

BILL [*in his sleep*]. Quack! Quack!

SPIELMANN. But I will tell you just one thing. I can safely say this because it applies to nearly everyone—

CLARA. Everyone! How *could* you, doctor!

SPIELMANN. It applies to nearly everyone but not in the same way. With a person of such unique sensibility as yours it naturally ensues that though the complaint is a common one, the manifestation of it is excessively, not to say fascinatingly, complicated. And that is why in your case, my dear, I shall be unable to say very much for another six months—

37

CLARA. But can I afford another six months?

SPIELMANN. Do not make these jokes, my dear. If you cannot afford it, who can?

CLARA. That is just what I should like to know.

SPIELMANN. To return, if you insist on some immediate indication (and unscientific impatience is a delightfully feminine quality) some immediate indication as to the line of approach I am taking in respect of a preliminary diagnosis with regard to the premises, or it might be more scientific to call them the presupposed factors which condition (hypothetically of course) the nodus of balanced elements positive and negative apart from the assumption of which as subordinate causes working backwards as well as forwards—

BILL [*in his sleep*]. Topside, backside, chump-chop, tripe.

CLARA. Please, doctor, couldn't you put it more simply?

[*Noise without.* MRS. FREUDENBERG *bursts in.*]

MRS. FREUDENBERG. It's not fair! It's not fair!

SPIELMANN. Ah, my dear Mrs. Freudenberg, it is a pleasure to see you again.

MRS. FREUDENBERG. Dr. Spielmann, something terrible has happened.

SPIELMANN. In that case, Mrs. Freudenberg, no doubt you wish to begin a further analysis? Excuse me, please, Miss de Groot.

MRS. FREUDENBERG. No, doctor, that's just it. It's my husband.

SPIELMANN. Ah. Your husband wants an analysis?

MRS. FREUDENBERG. No, no. My husband doesn't approve of analysis. He says I've lost all my charm since I've been psycho-analysed.

CLARA. Dr. Spielmann, I thought this was *my* hour for consultation.

SPIELMANN [*aside to* CLARA]. My dear, please forgive me. I'll get rid of her in a moment.

MRS. FREUDENBERG. My husband says I've lost all my funny little ways.

SPIELMANN. Oh but that is patently untrue, Mrs. Freudenberg.

MRS. FREUDENBERG. You console me, doctor, but I want to ask you something.

SPIELMANN. Certainly, certainly. Anything I can do for you—

MRS. FREUDENBERG. Well, as a very, very great favour, doctor, could you give me back just a little bit of my Unconscious?

CLARA. Dr. Spielmann, I am feeling very faint. There is an unpleasant scent in the room.

MRS. FREUDENBERG. You see, I don't even have any dreams now.

CLARA. Dr. Spielmann!

MRS. FREUDENBERG. Dr. Spielmann!

BILL [*waking up with a yell*]. Dr. Spielmann!

SPIELMANN. Now, please, don't get excited, ladies. Miss de Groot, just one moment, please. Now Mrs. Freudenberg, I am very sorry indeed but I am already, as you see, in process of consultation with

this lady—no, no, Mrs. Freudenberg, of course, yes
—I can see you tomorrow, will that do?—but you
want something immediately—will you tell me in
my ear?—ah, if that's it!—Look, Mrs. Freudenberg,
here is a drawing-block, perhaps you could draw it
for me? Yes, you draw very nicely. A person of
your unique sensibility—

CLARA. What!

SPIELMANN. And now perhaps, my dear Mrs. Freudenberg, you had better go home and get to work at
once. And then your husband perhaps— [*He shows
her out.*]

CLARA. You said she had unique sensibility!

SPIELMANN. Unique? Oh, only comparatively unique,
my dear.

CLARA. Well, I don't like it.

SPIELMANN. Now to return to what I was saying—

CLARA. I don't want to hear it.

SPIELMANN. You don't want to hear the truth about
yourself?

CLARA. The truth?

SPIELMANN. Are you listening? Good. I will put it as
succintly as possible. You will understand that
this is only a very approximate kind of statement—
what I might call an asymptote. What you want
my dear—now please do not take offence, many
people suffer from this but no one in so charming a
fashion as yourself—what you want is to be a little
less . . . a little less intro . . . intro . . .

BILL. Introverted.

SPIELMANN. Introverted. Now, of course, that little failing—it is not really a failing, merely an idiom—is in your position very understandable. You are the World's Sweetheart.

CLARA. Please do not be vulgar, doctor. If I remember correctly there was a little ninny film actress they used to call that before the War.

SPIELMANN. Exclusive preoccupation with self—however charming, as in your case, that self may be—is liable, as we who study these things have now ascertained, to lead in the end to a not altogether desirable condition which is technically known as—you will forgive the word, it comes from the Greek—technically known as . . . curious, it just slips me for the moment. . . .

  What the devil's wrong with you, Bill? Are you asleep?

BILL. Narcissism.

SPIELMANN. Ah yes, narcissism. It comes from the Greek. Now, my dear, I'm not implying that you're a narcissist, but, if I may make the suggestion, it would do you, I think, no harm were you to canalise some of your energies in other directions and so relieve the excessive centripetal strain on your thoughts and emotions. Have a love affair, for instance.

CLARA. No, Dr. Spielmann, I couldn't have a love affair. It's contrary to my contract. Don't you know they bill me as the Modern Diana. Besides, love seems to me so untidy.

41

SPIELMANN. Well, I won't suggest anything which would upset your routine. Routine is a biological, not to say cosmic, principle. Let me see. If a love affair is out of the question what would you say to taking up some little hobby? Say gardening.

CLARA. Good God, Dr. Spielmann, my hands! Look!

SPIELMANN. Very nice indeed.

CLARA. Do you know these hands cost ten pounds a week per nail? The public demands it.

SPIELMANN. That rules out gardening. I suppose the same would apply to dog-breeding? Even Pekingese?

CLARA. My dear Dr. Spielmann, I am a dog-breeder already. At my house in Hampshire I have prize-winning specimens exquisitely housed, of the fifty leading breeds. At the last show of the Canine and Ancient I won forty-seven green tickets. My head kennelman is an ex-Vice-President of the Berlin Zoo.

SPIELMANN. I have it! Art! You must cultivate an interest in Art.

CLARA. I am an artist.

SPIELMANN. Oh-er-yes. I mean the other kind.

BILL [in cockney]. He means the *Fine* Arts.

SPIELMANN. Yes. Pictures and statues. You must become a collector, a connoisseur.

CLARA. But, doctor, haven't you ever heard of my collection? It's the finest private collection in Europe. And my collection in America is the finest private collection in America. All my buying is in the hands of accredited experts.

42

SPIELMANN. Have you ever chosen one of your pictures yourself?

CLARA. Of course not. I never look at them afterwards, you see.

SPIELMANN. Excellent. I have a little proposal to make. Could you tolerate my company for a little longer this afternoon? Good. Then this afternoon you will choose your first picture. You and I will go together to Lindenbaum's.

CLARA. If that's an auction, I won't come.

SPIELMANN. It is an auction. But you will come.

CLARA. I shan't.

SPIELMANN. Really? Well that's a pity.

BILL. Now's the time for a spot of suggestion.

SPIELMANN. Don't teach me my business.

BILL. Sore spot, eh? Only thing the doc can ever bring off.

SPIELMANN. My dear Miss de Groot—

BILL. Now 'e's off!

SPIELMANN. My dear Miss de Groot, if you don't want to go, we won't press the point. The time for our interview is now up. I myself shall go to Lindenbaum's Auction because there is something very interesting going to occur there. Something very, very interesting. Something to seduce the soul and excite the senses. Something to give a new bent to one's life, new power to one's elbow, a new Weltanschauung, new epoch, crusade, religious revival, biologic upheaval, fusion of the past, hope of the future. What we shall find at that auction will be

43

stronger than steel, more volatile than mercury, more serene than a statue of Buddha, sweeter than the nostalgia of German songs.

CLARA. All that at Lindenbaum's auction?

SPIELMANN. All that at Lindenbaum's auction.

CLARA. Then I will come too.

BILL. What did I tell you?

CLARA [*speaking as if under hypnosis*].

> I will come too, to find my hope.
> A green bird in green trees.
> Who knows what will happen, what manna fall
> > into my hands,
> Gold flowers form in the air or unbelievable music?
> [*Suddenly, in her old voice.*]

But I won't look at any of the pictures. I don't like looking at pictures. [*They begin putting on their coats, etc.*]

I have enough pictures already. A picture's not like a book. When you've got it, you have to hang it somewhere. If you haven't got a wall you have to build a new house. That idea of hanging always put me off pictures—

BILL [*sings*]. 'They call me Hanging Johnny—'

SPIELMANN. Shut up, you. [*Goes out with* CLARA.]

BILL. —'Away, boys, away.

> They call me Hanging Johnny,
> So hang, boys, hang!

CURTAIN

[Dr. Spielmann *reappears in front of* cur-
tain *and sings or recites the following.*]:
The oracle
   High between the cliffs,
The tripod over
   The mephitic cleft,
Or the sybil's cave
   Where the winds blow
The dead leaf answers
   To and fro:
Where shall we find truth in an oracle?

The oracle
   Among the talking oaks,
The flight of birds,
   The examination of guts,
Luck of the cards,
   Lines of the hand,
Call of the raven
   In a sallow land:
Where shall we find truth in an oracle?

[Dr. Spielmann *goes out.* Listener-In
marches in, L., *and stands to attention beside his*

radio. The ANNOUNCER *marches in, R., and stands to attention beside the microphone. They stand silently for a minute. Then, to a drum beat they make one a right, the other a left, turn and stand facing each other, still at attention.*]

LISTENER-IN. I only take what you can give.

RADIO-ANNOUNCER. I only give you what you want.

LISTENER-IN. You who supply the meaning.

RADIO-ANNOUNCER. You who supply the matter.

LISTENER-IN. Is it an important matter?

RADIO-ANNOUNCER. Is it an attractive meaning?

LISTENER-IN. Come to me, crystallise out of the air.

RADIO-ANNOUNCER. Hypocrite auditeur, mon semblable, mon frère.

> [*They march towards each other and embrace. Then they turn towards the audience.*]

BOTH. The news that blows around the streets
> Or vibrates over the air
> Whether it is rape, embezzlement or murder
> Seems frivolous, if not farcical, without dignity.
> Whereas the actual fact before it becomes news
> Is often tragic even when commonplace.
> The daily press gives neither laughter nor tears
> But the stage of life gives both.
> We wish to remind you that upon this stage
> Slapstick may turn to swordplay,
> The cottage flowers may give a sudden hiss
> The trees curve down their hands in heavy gloves—
> A malediction on the nape of the neck.
> We will tell you a little fable:

There was a picnic party in the eighteenth century
Strayed out of canvas with their lutes and beakers
And called among the rocks to the lady Echo
But Echo missed her cue
And instead of returning the same coin they gave
     her,
Phrases of music and gallant phrases,
Echo like a gorgon glared from the sudden rocks
And cried in a stony voice the one word 'Death'.
These possibilities should always be remembered
But for the moment let us go back to our farce.

ACT 1

SCENE III

[*A street. Outside a Tourist Agency. Throughout this scene wealthy people keep walking in and out of the T.A. without saying anything.* PORTRIGHT *is walking up and down, bumping into these people.*]

PORTRIGHT. She's late. Why doesn't she come—I'm
          sorry, sir—

    I suppose this is the right place.

    Look at all these lucky people—they're wealthy—

    Wagon-Lits—the smell of orange blossom—

    Oh I'm sorry, madam—

    Why should I always have to keep saying I'm
          sorry?

    Why doesn't Moll O'Hara come?

    She doesn't take me seriously—

    I ought to have more lines on my face.

    An artist should have the sort of face—I beg your
          pardon—

    The sort of face makes the passers-by know he's an
          artist.

    The artist is a spiritual Napoleon on St. Helena

Or like the Mona Lisa whose eyelids are a little tired.
He is older than the rocks on which he sits.
Old Andy Nock—I beg your pardon, madam—
Died of cirrhosis of the liver;
That was an artist's death!

[*Enter* MOLL O'HARA.]

MOLL. Hullo, sunshine!

PORTRIGHT. Oh hullo, Moll O'Hara.

MOLL. What are you thinking about? Your picture?

PORTRIGHT. Oh my picture! No, I wasn't thinking
about her.

MOLL. Her!

PORTRIGHT. I was thinking about the different ways of
dying. A man ought to die of something significant.

MOLL. I know one thing you won't die of.

PORTRIGHT. What?

MOLL. Overwork.

PORTRIGHT. You're always talking about work.
I have worked harder than any man.
Think of all the pictures I have scrapped—
Supposing I had sold each of them for fifty pounds?
And think of all the pictures I never started.
There's strength of character for you!

MOLL. Where?

PORTRIGHT. Money is a terrible temptation!
Look at these tourist agencies where money will buy
you distance,
Miles and miles of distance for your money.
O the Tourist Agencies with revolving doors and
marble floors,

D   49

Schedules of the White Star Blue Star Green Star
    Red Star Black Star lines,
This way for the belles of Andalusia and the gar-
    lands of Tahiti
And the steam of the Victoria Falls.
This way if you want to see the wonders of Yellow-
    stone Park,
The tomb of Tutankhamen or Gandhi sitting at his
    wheel,
The roof of the Sistine Chapel, the Great Wall of
    China,
If you want to commune with strange winds, the
    mistral or the Sahara sandstorm,
Or dip your fingers in holy rivers, Ganges or Oxus—
If only I could, if only I could—
Oh for the shrill hustle of the Gare de Lyon,
The swallows flying south, the moneyed swallows.
MOLL. Romanticist!
    What you want is some good earthy contacts.
PORTRIGHT. Earthy contacts? Haven't I enough al-
    ready?
Running the gauntlet of uncontrolled reactions,
Facing the barrage of the daily light of the sun
And the rape of summer flowers upon my eyes and
    nostrils,
Stabbed with tulips, trench-mortared with peonies,
Buried in the velvet dark under the scent of vio-
lets—
    [*A very fat man bumps into him and knocks him
    down.*]

50

MOLL. Earthy contacts!

Look, my dear, let me get that mud off your cheek.

Now we'll be off to find your picture.

PORTRIGHT. Will it be at the auction?

MOLL. Yes, Lindenbaum's auction. Half-an-hour's time.

PORTRIGHT. But how can we buy it? We have no money.

MOLL [*opening her bag*]. Look here.

PORTRIGHT. And you dunned me for ten guineas!

MOLL. You ought to be like me—

Have an eye to the main drain.

PORTRIGHT. No, I could never be like you—

That is not to your discredit, of course—

I know all about myself—

MOLL. You have thought a lot about yourself?

PORTRIGHT. Yes. A great deal.

Concentration on self is the necessary preliminary—

MOLL. Listen to me, Portright my dear.

All this concentration on self

Means in the end a mutilation of self.

You are a dilettante, you draw up a lovely menu

And you poison yourself.

PORTRIGHT. If it is poison, let the poison be precise—

Excuse me, sir; excuse me, madam—

Have you ever seen a picture of St. John with a gold cup in his hand

And a tiny viper flowering out of the cup?

MOLL. Come along, we must be going.

PORTRIGHT. A tiny viper.

51

MOLL. We will go to Lindenbaum's by Underground.

PORTRIGHT. Oh no, I couldn't do that.

MOLL. Why not?

PORTRIGHT. I've got a phobia about it.

MOLL. About what?

PORTRIGHT. About the Underground.

MOLL. What's wrong with the Underground?

PORTRIGHT. Why, it's under ground.

MOLL. Well, that's the way things are, you know. A
thing is what it is. A thing wouldn't be called underground if it was up in the sky.

PORTRIGHT. There is no freedom in this world.

> [*He postures as if to declaim.*]

MOLL. Oh no, you've done enough of that.
I'll talk a bit of poetry now.

> [*She comes forward and addresses the audi-
ence.*]

The dog stares into the fire, beatitude of platitude,
God be praised that things are as they are,
That grass is green, that water is wet, that trees are
tall,
That every man is always out for himself,
That boss is boss, bantam is bantam, mascot is mas-
cot,
That pistons rise and fall, that prices rise and fall,
that wheels go round in wheels,
That people are different from each other
And people are the same as each other
And people are different from themselves
And people are the same as themselves

52

And God be praised that in the shaft of the sun
The motes of dust keep dancing.

    And now, my dear, you're coming with me on the
Underground.
> [*She takes his arm and leads him off. Two or three
> newsboys run on to the stage shouting '3.30
> Special! Breakdown of Peace Conference! Break-
> down of Peace Conference!' The people coming
> out of the Tourist Agency buy papers. The* FAT
> MAN *comes out last and buys a paper.*]

FAT MAN [*having studied the paper very solemnly*]. So
much for my trip round the world! [*He opens his
pocket book, takes out a ticket, walks to the front of the
stage, tears up the ticket and sprinkles the pieces
among the* ORCHESTRA.]

        CURTAIN

[The LISTENER-IN *and the* RADIO-ANNOUNCER
come on before the CURTAIN *and sing or recite.*]:
Riding in cars
On tilting roads
We have left behind
Our household gods,
We have left behind
The cautious clause,
The laws of the over-
rational mind.

Frost on the window,
Skater's figures,
Gunmen fingering
Anxious triggers,
Stocks and shares
(The ribbon of the rich),
The favourite down
At the blind ditch.

Forgotten now
The early days,
Youth's idyllic
And dawdling ways;

Cruising along
   On the long road
We do not notice
   The limping god.

Swinging between
   Crutches he comes
To an overture
   Of buried drums;
His eyes will turn
   Our hands to stone,
His name is Time,
   He walks alone.

Our world is built on buying and selling,
Mortgaged mansions and bargain basements.
All who have money are buying and selling.
So come to the auction, come to the auction,
You never know what you may find,
Some masterpiece may be going cheap:
A lamp, an ointment, or a sword,
A saintly relic or a magic word.

ACT I

SCENE IV

[*Auction Room. A neo-Gothic hall.* COLLECTORS *ranged in tiers right and left. They are talking to each other in many languages. Enter* MISS HASKEY *with a* COMMISSIONAIRE.]

COMMISSIONAIRE. Here you are, Miss. Sit anywhere you like.

MISS H. Can I sit here?

COMMISSIONAIRE. Anywhere you like, Miss. You've never been to an auction before?

MISS H. Oh no, I never go out much. I am only here for a purpose. I have heard that a picture painted by a dear friend of mine is going to be disposed of this afternoon.

COMMISSIONAIRE. A deceased friend, eh?

MISS H. Well, not quite deceased—

COMMISSIONAIRE. Poor fellow!

They fetch a good price, the things here.

MISS H. Oh, do they? I am sorry to hear that. I have only got my savings, you see—

COMMISSIONAIRE. Well, miss, I must be going. The

best of luck. Beginner's luck, you know. You may get it cheap.

[*Goes out. Organ music. The* AUCTIONEER *enters, in a surplice.*]

AUCTIONEER. Ladies and gentlemen, good day.

Let us pass a few moments in silent prayer.

[*Pause. The* COLLECTORS *bow their heads.*]

Ladies and gentlemen,

I have the privilege today to bring before you the entire collection of the late Mr. Greenough-Leonides—

That great man—

Also various sundries from other sources.

Before entering upon the performance of my solemn duty—

And I only pray that these objects will fall into the right hands—

I should like to say a few words about the late Mr. Greenough-Leonides—

That great man!

The late Mr. Greenough-Leonides was born a millionaire

But from his birth he was deaf, dumb and blind.

Finding himself in that position he did not give up the struggle

But set himself to the task of improving the world:

He became one of the greatest collectors of all time.

His taste was exquisite.

Shortly before his death—

57

[*Enter self-consciously* DR. SPIELMANN *and*
CLARA DE GROOT. *All the* COLLECTORS *turn
to look at them.*]

COLLECTORS. Sh! Sh!

CLARA. What an odd smell, Dr. Spielmann.

SPIELMANN. I think we'll sit here, my dear. You must
keep quiet now. The gentleman is speaking.

AUCTIONEER. I regret that there has been an interrup-
tion. It is not the first time I have had to speak to
members of this congregation about this habit of
coming in late.

    We should all remember where we are when we
        meet beneath these arches—
    'Take your shoes from off your feet for this is
        holy ground'.

                [MISS HASKEY *takes off her shoes.*]

    What is it we do here, you and I in communion?
    Here we appraise the relics of time and the works
        of genius,
    The only palpable forms of communication
        among men.
    Regard therefore your purchases as an offering to
        God
    Or a tribute on the altar of human aspirations,
    A token of the defiant creativeness of Man.

    [*Pause. Organ music. Enter* MOLL O'HARA *and*
    PORTRIGHT. *They sit down on the opposite side
    of the stage to* CLARA *and* SPIELMANN.]

MOLL. My God, there's your housekeeper!

PORTRIGHT. Where? Yes, so she is. But where's Venus?

58

Moll. Sh! You'll give the show away.

Auctioneer. Before bringing under the hammer the
      Greenough-Leonides collection itself
I have some comparatively less important items—
The first of these is the life-size figure of an elephant
      in Hoptonwood Stone by the world-famous
      artist Stein Mac Stein.
This will be put up for sale in the adjoining room.
Will all interested please follow me.

      [*He moves out to organ music followed by the*
      Collectors *and* Miss Haskey. *Only* Moll,
      Portright, Clara *and* Spielmann *remain.*]

Clara. Dr. Spielmann, I don't think I can stay here. It
      is the atmosphere.

Spielmann. You are so sensitive, my dear. But just
      wait and things will become exciting.

Clara. And what is so extraordinary, none of these
      people seem to recognise me.

Spielmann. They are mostly foreigners.

Clara. Foreigners! But my films are shown every-
      where.

Spielmann. That little man over there is looking at
      you.

Clara. One little man! What is that?

Moll. Patience, my dear, patience.

Portright. My picture!
      Isn't that Clara de Groot?

Moll. Yes. Talk of the devil. We were talking of her,
      you remember.

Portright. She *is* beautiful, you know.

59

MOLL. So is an icicle.

SPIELMANN. They're staring very properly now.

CLARA. Who are they, do you think?

SPIELMANN. Types, my dear, that's all they are.
Types of individualists.

MOLL. Look there. Under the black velvet. I have a
hunch that's your Venus.

PORTRIGHT. Yes. [*He goes on staring at* CLARA.]

[*Organ march. The* COLLECTORS *re-enter and
sing their hymn. Then* AUCTIONEER *enters; he
is now in his shirt-sleeves and has taken on a
much brisker personality.*]

HYMN OF THE COLLECTORS

Spring comes with drums and jonquils
    And smells of French fern soap
And telephones keep ringing
    Insistent bells of hope;
Some gather New Year honours
    Enrolled as knight or bart
And some like us pay homage
    Before the shrines of Art.

Then gather all ye faithful
    Combined against the foe,
The philistine and film-fan,
    The bitch, the hog, the crow.
They snuffle in their nosebags,
    They drag the hangman's cart
But we will hold our noses
    And cull the fruits of Art.

60

So gather in this precinct
        Before the days grow worse
With reverence on your eyelids
        And money in your purse;
And since the cheque for thousands
        Reveals the contrite heart
Bid high the fancy prices
        Of priceless works of Art.

AUCTIONEER. Now then, ladies and gentlemen, look
    alive now.
    That was a nice piece of work and a real bargain for
    the lady who purchased it.
                                    [*To* MISS HASKEY.]
    May I congratulate you once more,
    Madam. [*He studies a list.*]
MOLL. Good God, she's bought the elephant.
                            [*Goes over to* MISS HASKEY.]
    Miss Haskey!
MISS H. I am not speaking to you.
MOLL. Now, now, Miss Haskey. Please.
MISS H. [*beginning to cry*]. Oh dear, oh dear, I've done
    it now.
MOLL. What have you done?
MISS H. I came here to buy the picture for Mr. Port-
    right.
    And now . . . and now . . .
    Something ran away with me and I spent it all on
    the elephant.
MOLL. Never mind, dear. It'll all be all right.

AUCTIONEER. Silence! [MOLL *rejoins* PORTRIGHT.]
>Before us now we have an assortment of objects,
>Objects to warm the cockles of the heart of every
>>born collector,
>As dear as the smell of beans in May or bonfires in
>>October,
>As dear as the feel of your best girl's hand gloved in
>>delicate suede,
>As dear as the splash of waves on a boat when you
>>lie in your cabin and steam for home—

VOICE. We don't want 'em dear, we want 'em cheap.

AUCTIONEER [*pontifically again*]. Remember where
you are, please.

>>>>>[*Briskly again.*]
>First we have this collection of old ivory.

>>>>>[*Sings.*]

>>Who'll buy my ivory, ivory, old ivory
>>Who'll buy my ivory
>>>At five o'clock in the morning?

COLLECTORS [*sing*].

>>We'll buy his ivory, ivory, ivory,
>>>Buy his bloody old ivory
>>>At five o'clock in the morning.

AUCTIONEER.

>>What'll you give for me ivory, ivory, ivory,
>>What'll you give for me ivory
>>>At five o'clock in the morning?

COLLECTORS

>>We'll give you a curse for your ivory,
>>>ivory, ivory,

We'll give you a curse for your ivory
At five o'clock in the morning.

AUCTIONEER. Done! Walk up here please one at a time. Old ivory whatnots one curse per item. This way, sir. This way, madam. Here you are. Nice old ivory toothpicks.

[*The* COLLECTORS *file past to the sound of the hammer, each receiving his object and saying in turn:*

Dash!

Hang!

Blast!

Damn!

Sqtsk!

Ooch!

Pff! *etc. etc.*]

AUCTIONEER. The next item, ladies and gentlemen, is behind this velvet cover. This is what we call the surprise packet. Mark what I say for I have not much time to say it.

Not much time.

[*Suddenly becoming very excited.*]

Ladies and gentlemen, time is running out,
Time like an elephant has thrown his
     mahout,
Time is out of hand, is lumbering about,
Buy while you may before he runs out.

[*Conversationally.*]

Now I don't think I'll let you see this work till you've bought it.

This picture is the immaculate work of a master
artist—

MOLL. That's you dearie. Couldn't be anyone else.

AUCTIONEER. Silence there, silence!

This picture is the master work of an immaculate
artist—

CLARA. The papers say that I am immaculate. It's the
same as being Diana.

AUCTIONEER. Silence! Silence!

This picture is the work of an artist.

There is no reserve price.

Any offers any offers for this astounding creation,

The only piece that its author has ever completed—

MOLL. It *is* you.

AUCTIONEER. A magnum opus, the only one of its kind.

Any offers, any offers, going for a song,

Going for a gob of spittle, a snap of the fingers,

Going for an oath on the Bible or a promise of eter-
nal love,

Going for a song, for a glass dog's chance,

Going for a pinch of snuff, a medal of service,

Going for a packet of mummy wheat, going for a
cure for cancer,

Going for Lancashire cotton, going for bodyline
bowling,

Going for a syllogism, going for a nostrum, going for
a dream of golden horses—

Any offers for this picture of the Rising Venus,

The work of a master, the chance of a lifetime?

VOICE. I'll offer half a guinea.

AUCTIONEER. Half a guinea. I am offered half a guinea for the Rising Venus.

Any advance on half a guinea.

MOLL. One guinea.

SPIELMANN. Two guineas.

MOLL. Three guineas.

SPIELMANN. I'll fix *her*.

Three guineas and a course of psycho-analysis.

VOICE. Three guineas and a prayer every day to St. Joseph.

SPIELMANN. That is not an advance.

AUCTIONEER. I am offered three guineas and a prayer every day to St. Joseph. Any advance on—

MOLL. Three guineas and a shooting stick. It's quite new. I got it for Christmas.

AUCTIONEER. I am offered three guineas and a shooting stick. It is quite new. She got it for Christmas.

SPIELMANN. This is ridiculous.

CLARA. Go on, doctor, go on.

VOICE. Three guineas and a black cat neuter.

MOLL. That's easy. Three guineas and a black cat.

CLARA. Bid something, doctor.

SPIELMANN. My dear, I have bid my best. A course—

AUCTIONEER. I am offered three guineas and a black cat for the Rising Venus.

SPIELMANN. Now can't *you* bid anything, my dear?

What have you got which no one else has?

CLARA. Money.

SPIELMANN. They don't seem to be bothering about money.

E   65

CLARA. Well, beauty.

SPIELMANN. You can't *give* your beauty, you know.

AUCTIONEER. Any advance on three guineas and a black cat.

SPIELMANN. I know; your autograph.

CLARA. I offer three guineas and my autograph.

AUCTIONEER. What is your name, please, madam?

CLARA. My name! My name!

SPIELMANN. Her name is Clara de Groot, the world-famous actress.

MOLL. That's sunk us.

AUCTIONEER. Clara de Groot. All right. Any advance on three guineas and the autograph of Miss Clara de Groot? Come now, ladies and gentlemen, any advance? I am offered three guineas and the autograph of Miss Clara de Groot for this picture of the Rising Venus. Going, going—your last chance, ladies and gentlemen, your last chance to purchase this lasting adornment for your homes, this bijou masterpiece, this *sine qua non* of a cultivated epoch, going, going, going; going like smoke from a chimney or water under the bridges, going like the dream of a shadow to which the poet of Thebes compared the existence of man, going like the loves of adolescence, going like the happiness of hashish, going like the tide at its turn or the ski-jumper poised on the brink or the bomb when the pin has been extracted or a spell of dry weather in Ireland or the life of a grouse at a shoot of the Duke of Calmyre, going, going, going, going—

66

[*Sings*]. Ach du lieber Augustin, Augustin, Augustin—any more offers, ladies and gentlemen, any more offers, knaves and fools, crooks, pimps, sluts and zanies, any more offers for this nonsense? No, no more offers? Not the least little shadow of the fraction of an eyelash, not the twentieth decimal place in—

All right then. Going: going: going: gone. Knocked down to this lady here for the sum of three guineas and her own autograph. [*Uproar and Cheers.*]

CLARA. Doctor, I have won!

SPIELMANN. Congratulations, my dear.

I wonder what the damn thing looks like.

PORTRIGHT. Oh hell!

MOLL. It's all right, my dear, we haven't lost yet.

MISS H. [*coming up*]. I am so sorry, Mr. Portright. I would have bid if I could.

MOLL. We must keep a watch on our friend, Miss de Groot. If it comes to the worst, we will burgle her flat.

AUCTIONEER. Now, Miss de Groot, do you wish to remove the picture immediately?

CLARA. What do I say, doctor? I don't really want the picture.

SPIELMANN. Miss de Groot will take the picture with her now.

CLARA. You are so dominating, Dr. Spielmann.

AUCTIONEER. In that case, sir, you are free to come and remove it. But first by your leave, for the benefit of the distinguished persons present, I would like

67

to unveil the work in question so that all may have the satisfaction of seeing what they have failed to buy.

MOLL. They'll be satisfied all right.

[*The crowd surge round the dais in expectation.*]

CLARA. What a crowd, doctor! I feel faint.

SPIELMANN. That is all right, my dear.

CLARA. We'll never get out of the door.

MOLL. What about snaffling it in the crowd?

CLARA. Doctor, I must have air.

SPIELMANN. Well, we can't go without the picture.

CLARA. Damn the picture.

AUCTIONEER. I am now about to unveil the Rising Venus.

SPIELMANN. Just a moment please, sir.

[*To* CLARA.]

You have heard of suggestion? It is an art at which I have some slight experience. I am going to try an experiment. I'll fix this crowd for you.

AUCTIONEER. Well, what do you want to say?

SPIELMANN. Before you unveil the picture, I wish to make a speech. [*Cheers.*]

AUCTIONEER. All right. Go ahead.

SPIELMANN [*putting on a fixed glare and a peculiar voice*]. Ladies and gentlemen, this picture which has been bought by Miss de Groot is no ordinary picture.

PORTRIGHT. Hear, hear!

SPIELMANN. It is as you know, a picture of the Rising Venus. It happens to have been painted by a man dying of an incurable disease—

MOLL. That's news for you, dearie.

68

AUCTIONEER. It doesn't say that in my catalogue.

SPIELMANN. Painting it under those circumstances he put into it the whole of his life. He was a man who had been a very great lover. He wished his picture to preach what he had practised. He wished his picture to be a missionary for love. [*Cheers.*] He was successful. This picture of his, this last will and testament of a lover, is endowed with a magical function which in a moment you will see exemplified. For do you know what is going to happen to you? The moment that this picture is unveiled, every person in this room who looks at the picture is going to fall in love. Every male person present will fall in love with some one female person present and vice versa. I would add, in case you do not know it, that next door to these rooms there is a nice little dance hall where the loving couples could conveniently adjourn. That is all and I congratulate you all in advance.

VOICE. The man is mad.

AUCTIONEER. Shall I unveil now?

SPIELMANN. Certainly.

    [*To Clara.*] You watch what happens.

CLARA. I'm not going to look. I don't look at pictures anyway.

PORTRIGHT. I'm not going to look. Not till she belongs to me again.

        [AUCTIONEER *unveils the picture.*]

ALL. Ooh!

MOLL [*having stared at the picture for some time and looking at* PORTRIGHT]. So that's it, is it?

69

[*The* COLLECTORS *jump up, pair off equally according to sex and embrace. Dance music strikes up, they waltz round the stage and out,* MISS HASKEY *pairing with the* AUCTIONEER. *Only* MOLL, PORTRIGHT, CLARA *and* SPIELMANN *remain.* SPIELMANN *goes up on the dais and begins covering up the picture again.*]

CLARA. Doctor, you are wonderful!

SPIELMANN. Oh, that's nothing, my dear. I thought they would be a suggestible lot.

CLARA. What is the picture like?

SPIELMANN. Nothing much, I am afraid.

PORTRIGHT. The swine!

MOLL. Hush, darling.

CLARA. Have you fallen in love with anyone, doctor?

SPIELMANN. Me? No. Why should I?

Come now. We must take this to your flat.

CLARA. I must say. Auctions are quite exciting. [*She goes out with* SPIELMANN.]

PORTRIGHT. What are we to do now?

MOLL. After them, darling, after them.

PORTRIGHT. Why do you call me darling?

MOLL. Why not?

You know, that picture of yours—

PORTRIGHT. Yes?

MOLL. It has its points after all.

Come on.

[*They go out.*]

CURTAIN

70

[MOLL O'HARA *speaks before the* CURTAIN.]

MOLL. Falling in love is nothing in itself,
    It is merely a stick got jammed across a stream,
    And other sticks and bits of floating stuff
    Get tangled with it and leaves and mud silt up
    Till the course of the stream is broken if not
        stopped.
    Or if you prefer a larger simile
    Compare it to the timber rivers of Canada
    When all the logs get jammed and men are crushed
        to death.
    It all begins with an incident, an odd chance,
    Or merely a hoax like this.
    The centre of any circle is merely a point,
    It is the circumference that matters.
    Falling in love gives daily life an orbit,
    Orientates our hackwork and necessities.
    In the same way the sexual act is almost nothing,
    An evanescent, intense, but frivolous pleasure,
    The mere caprice of an electric spark
    Which jinks a tiny gap and builds a bridge for
        armies.
    So much for falling in love and the act of love
71

But the same is true, or almost, of the beloved.
Whom you love is comparatively unimportant,
Any tree or shrub will give you a line on the land-
    scape.
But do not think I say this cynically.
The world runs at hazard, we must counterfeit,
Affect to copy the world, let chance do all it likes,
Give whom it will for parents or for lovers,
Mark out the field with accidental landmarks,
And we will do the rest.
Action is the cream of life and we will act
By our own rules on any stage we strike.

ACT II

ACT II

[*Before the* CURTAIN. LISTENER-IN'S *chair, L. Microphone, R.*

Enter simultaneously LISTENER-IN, *who sits down in chair, and* RADIO-ANNOUNCER *who stands before microphone.* RADIO-ANNOUNCER *looks round him on the floor, searches in his pockets and then, with an inspiration, puts his hand in the microphone and produces a coloured ball, which he bounces once or twice on the floor.*]

RADIO-ANNOUNCER [*throwing ball to* LISTENER-IN, *who jumps up and catches it*]. Hullo there!

LISTENER-IN [*throwing back ball*]. Hullo!

RADIO-ANNOUNCER [*throwing back ball*]. Can you catch what I say?

LISTENER-IN [*throwing back ball*]. Yes.

[*During the following conversation each man throws the ball across to the other on beginning a remark. Meanwhile they approach each other.*]

RADIO-ANNOUNCER. Do you mind if I speak to you direct for a moment?

LISTENER-IN. With pleasure.

75

RADIO-ANNOUNCER. Then a word in your ear, my friend.

LISTENER-IN. Well?

RADIO-ANNOUNCER. I'm going to be out of a job soon.

LISTENER-IN. Why?

RADIO-ANNOUNCER. Because the wireless is going to be appropriated for military purposes. Its function in future will be not pleasure but utility.

LISTENER-IN. I am sorry for that.

RADIO-ANNOUNCER. And another word in your ear, my friend.

LISTENER-IN. Yes?

RADIO-ANNOUNCER. You are going to be out of a seat soon.

LISTENER-IN. What seat?

RADIO-ANNOUNCER. That study chair of yours.
They won't let you hang on to that.

> [LISTENER-IN *does not answer but backs quickly towards his chair.*]

Hi! did you catch what I said?
It was a warning.

LISTENER-IN [*throwing back ball*]. Take your damn warning. I'm going to sit in my chair while I have time.

> [LISTENER-IN *sits down again.* RADIO-ANNOUNCER *returns to the microphone.*]

RADIO-ANNOUNCER [*into microphone*]. Hm!

> [*Throwing ball across to* LISTENER-IN.]

Get a move on there. Turn the bloody knob.

LISTENER-IN [*pocketing the ball*]. Oh no I don't. I'm not listening in this evening.

76

RADIO-ANNOUNCER. I can't hear what you say.

     Do you hear what I say?

        [LISTENER-IN *makes no sign of understanding.*]

     Well, that's torn it. No listeners, no radio.

          [*He sits down disconsolately on the floor.*]

LISTENER-IN. I think it's my turn to talk.

        [*He goes across to the microphone and puts the
        ball into it.*]

Ladies and gentlemen,

My talk this evening is entitled 'Summer is
    A-Comen In'.

You needn't listen if you don't want to.

Summer is a-Comen in. Soon we must change the
    clocks,

Give up our coal fire, fill the grate with lilac,

Mow the lawn and clip the hawthorn hedge,

Take longer spins in the car,

Stud the radiator with wasps and flies,

And smell the good new tar upon the road,

Plant out the geraniums from the potting shed,

Take part in the office sweepstake on the Derby,

Buy a new panama, read about the County Cricket

But never watch it—it takes up too much time—

Read about Wimbledon, Henley and Ascot.

Read the advertisements for seaside lodgings,

Bungalows to let and Mediterranean cruises.

This is the type of the English summer.

But will this summer run true to type?

The official announcers would never mention them

But there are certain factors to be considered.

First, there is a war about to be declared.
Second—but who cares about the second?
Summer is a-Comen in. If there is war,
What sort of summer will it be?
Will there be any green grass left at Lord's?
Will there be any horses to run at Ascot?
Will there be any brass bands to meet the return-
ing heroes
Supposing any return?
　　When the heroes came back from the ten years'
　　　　war
　　(But no war now will last ten years)
　　They struck a port they seemed to have seen
　　　　before.
　　There were old men sitting on the bollards
　　Puffing smoke across the sea,
　　There were dead men hanging in the gantries,
　　There was a lame bird limping on the quay.
　　When were we here before? one of them said.
　　The captain answered: This is where we were
　　　　born
　　And where we have now returned. Dead to the
　　　　Dead.
Summer is a-Comen in. A packet of sunflower seed
To plant along the wall. A packet of Sweet William.
What else, my dear? The children like it, you know,
To have some flowers of their own.
They like a little garden to look after—
　　　　　　[*Echo off.* After, after—]
And what comes after that?

78

Flowers in the sky, rockets and flares.
Things are not what they were, the time is past
For growing in a quiet plot,
For sleeping in an easy bed.

> [*The clock strikes and the* ANNOUNCER *leaps up.*]

RADIO-ANNOUNCER. Excuse me, old man, you did
  very well,
But it was all very out of order.
Now we must get back to routine.
You go back to your chair and listen to this.

> [LISTENER-IN *returns to his chair and turns on his radio set.*]

Good evening, everybody. I am going to intro-
duce to you this evening Mr. MacDonald, the famous
veteran low hurdler, who is going to give you a
short talk on the subject of the forthcoming
Olympic Games, which are due to commence this
day week in the Gran Chaco. Mr. MacDonald!

> [*Takes three steps back and forward again and speaks in a Scotch accent.*]

Ladies and gentlemen. The primary problem
which arises before us when we consider the subject of the Olympic Games is who, if any, are the
nations which are going to be the competitors.
This year the world is in a very troubled state but I
think I can say with confidence that it has been as
troubled before, aye, and that it will be even more
troubled again. This being so, I cannot, after giving
all due consideration to the subject, endorse the

opinion of those pessimists who hold that the Olympic Games are a thing of the past. Now I, ladies and gentlemen, have the artistic temperament and I cannot believe in pessimism. Once upon a time I visited Olympia in Greece. Strolling up and down that old-world spot I thought to myself: what a wonderful thought it is that nothing changes in the world except Progress. Those old Greeks were very talented men both mentally and physically but they lacked something. They lacked the idea of Progress, the idea which has brought the modern world to where it stands today. Now about these Olympic Games. You know, of course, that our own great country is unfortunately unable to compete this year; the grounds of this decision are political, economic and military and are, therefore, not open to criticism. The same is true of the Dominions of the British Empire, of Japan, the United States, and all the great powers of Europe. The South American republics are also non-competitors, it being their contention that if the Olympic Games were to be held in South America at all they ought to have been held somewhere else than in the Gran Chaco. There is something in this point of view. Who then, you will ask, are the remaining competitors. This question I shall be in a position to answer next week, by which time I shall have given the most careful consideration to every side of the question. By this day next week the Gran Chaco will be gay with bunting and resounding to the fall

80

of the hammer and the weight and the merry chink of the spikes in the running-shoes of the athletes. That is all I am in a position to say to you this evening but there is a young man here at my elbow who is going to read you aloud a poem appropriate to the subject in praise of the great Greek athlete Pindar, a statue of whom stands, as we all know, in our own Piccadilly Circus. Mr.—what did you say your name was—Mr. Smith.

[RADIO-ANNOUNCER *steps back and forward again and recites as Smith.*]

There are hikers on all the roads—
    Pindar is dead—
The petrol pumps are doing a roaring business,
Motors are tuning up for the Easter races,
Building companies are loaning to the newly
    married—
    Pindar is dead and that's no matter.
There are climbers on all the hills—
    Pindar is dead—
With oiled boots and ropes they are tackling
    Snowdon,
The swimming-baths are filled for Easter Monday,
Doctored with chlorine to prevent infection—
    Pindar is dead and that's no matter.

There is money on all the horses—
    Pindar is dead—
One belongs to a proud and a plethoric peer,
One to a maharajah, one to a midland magnate,

One to a dago count and one to a tweeded spin-
    ster—
Pindar is dead and that's no matter.

There are flowers in all the markets—
Pindar is dead—
Daffodils, tulips, and forced roses,
New potatoes and green peas for Easter,
Wreaths of moss and primrose for the churches
But no wreaths for runners, whether of olive or
    laurel—
Pindar is dead and that's no matter.
    [RADIO-ANNOUNCER *steps away from the
    microphone, mops his forehead and throws the
    ball to* LISTENER-IN.]

RADIO-ANNOUNCER. Hullo there! How did you like
that?

LISTENER-IN. I didn't think much of that.

RADIO-ANNOUNCER. You people are very hard to
please.

I say!

LISTENER-IN. Yes?

RADIO-ANNOUNCER. This may be our last night in
partnership. Could you give a chap a drink?

LISTENER-IN. Delighted to, my dear fellow. [*Produces
a bottle of whisky from beside his chair.*]

RADIO-ANNOUNCER. Our last night in partnership—
You the listener and me the talker!
    [*They link arms in the middle of the stage and
    drink.*]

82

LISTENER-IN. You think the world's really coming to an end?

RADIO-ANNOUNCER. Sure! well, when I say the world—

LISTENER-IN. You mean you and me?

RADIO-ANNOUNCER. That's it.

LISTENER-IN. Have another drink?

RADIO-ANNOUNCER. Many thanks. One gets thirsty being a voice.

[They both drink.]

LISTENER-IN. How does that poem run? You would know.

RADIO-ANNOUNCER. What poem?

LISTENER-IN. You know. What's become of something?

RADIO-ANNOUNCER. What's become of what?

LISTENER-IN. That's what I want to know.

RADIO-ANNOUNCER. If you can't remember, make it up.

LISTENER-IN. All right. But you help me.

[They declaim.]

What's become of all the glory and the grandeur of
the gold-men and the gunmen,
The long breakers topped with silver of expanding
power and profits,
Of the well-upholstered mansion, seven flights of
stairs for the servants
Carrying coal from six in the morning?
What's become of the squadron of butlers, valets,
grooms and second housemaids?
Gone like the carriage-horse and cabhorse that once
dunged the streets of London.

83

What's become of the oracles in beards and whis-
    kers, beauty in bustles?
What's become of Mr. Gladstone or of grandpa's
    roll-top desk,
Waterloo Bridge and General Gordon?
What's become of them? What's becoming of us?
Look ahead, Long-Sighted Jim,
What do you see in the future dim?
    I look ahead and what do I see?
    I see a pageant, a Lord Mayor's procession,
    The Aldermen and the flunkeys, the carnival
        giants,
    The tableaux on lorries, the flags and the coaches,
    And every single one of the people who make
        that procession
    Carries a white stick to show that he is blind.
What's become of the light of day, the golden
    spokes of the sun's wheels,
What's become of the fingers of light that picked
    the locks of the dark places,
What's become of all our private sentinels?
    Answer: The sentry has gone.
    He will not come back.
    The pavement was worn by his feet
    But moss will grow over the tracks.
    Anyone now can approach
    The door of your house without fear.
    The burglar, the beggar, the drunk,
    The murdering madman, the whore,
    The prophet in sackcloth, the priest,

84

The jackal, the tiger, the snake,
All have their eye on your door.
CHORUS [*off.*] Close all the doors, bar all the shutters,
Be ready with revolver and electric torch,
Fire extinguisher and telephone directory,
Bible, cheque book and *savoir faire*:
The vultures are gathered together,
Their hooked wings carve the urban air.
When the golden cycle is over, the wise men said,
Fire will consume the lot, the game resume,
And feathers of the birds of prey will singe as they
tear the prey,
And the corpses roast where they fell
And the small blue flames will play
Like kittens with a ball of wool . . .
FIRE FIRE FIRE FIRE . . .
Fire in Troy, fire in Babylon, fire in Nineveh, fire in
London,
FIRE FIRE FIRE FIRE
The buckets are empty of water, the hoses are
punctured,
The city main is cut off, the holy well is dry,
There is no succour in the dusty ground, the metal-
lic sky,
No rock will spout with water at the prophet's rod,
Nor fate repeat the legendary flood,
There is nothing to stem the mechanical march of
fire,
Nothing to assuage the malice of the drunken fire.
FIRE FIRE FIRE FIRE

ACT II

SCENE I

[CLARA DE GROOT'S *flat. About one-third of the stage from the left the stage is divided by a wall which is a light screen on rollers. To L. of this is* CLARA'S *bedroom, to the R. a sitting-room. Extreme R., a wall juts out diagonally towards L., revealing about five square feet of landing outside the door to the sitting-room. A screen and a cupboard. On one wall hangs a picture with a bracket-light over it. Enter* CLARA *with* DR. SPIELMANN *carrying the picture.*]

SPIELMANN. Here we are.

CLARA [*wearily*]. Here we are.

SPIELMANN. Now what shall we do with the pretty picture?

CLARA. Oh, hang the picture!

SPIELMANN. An excellent proposal, my dear. Shall we try it up here in place of the Daumier? The light is so convenient.

CLARA. Oh, I am so tired.

SPIELMANN. You sit down, my dear. This will improve the room. The other was too gloomy.

86

CLARA. I am so tired.

SPIELMANN. One should not have gloomy things in one's rooms. A great artist, of course, Daumier, but morbid.

CLARA. I feel strange tonight.

SPIELMANN. You are tired after the excitement.

CLARA. What excitement? Oh the auction, you mean?

SPIELMANN. You must admit, however, that you enjoyed it.

CLARA. No, doctor. They were too rough at the end. When they all ran out with each other.

SPIELMANN. Ah that was my little trick. The gift of suggestion.

CLARA. Well, I wish you wouldn't do things like that. Making them all fall in love with each other. It's not as if they were your patients.

SPIELMANN. Oh it won't do them any harm. But I know your ideas on the subject.

CLARA. I think it's odious. And I'm so tired I could scream.

SPIELMANN. Shall I turn the wireless on for you? You will find it restful. [*He turns it on.*]

RADIO VOICE. Special News Bulletin: The time is now 21.35. The peace Conference is still in session at Geneva but the governments of the different countries are expected to withdraw their representatives at any minute. At the adjournment for afternoon tea this afternoon, little hope was expressed of a satisfactory solution being arrived at. In the opinion of experts the declaration of war by at least five if not more of the leading nations is imminent within the next twenty-four hours. Details of today's discussion are not yet available for publication but half a dozen white papers and blue papers will, it is hoped, be issued within a month or two. Armies are reported to be massing on the Volga, the Rhine, the Rhone, the Danube, the White and Blue Niles, and the Yangtze Kiang. The political situation has had the following effect upon world markets.

> [DR. SPIELMANN *turns it down very low. A Stock Exchange report is just audible during the following remarks.*]

CLARA. What did he say? The effect on the markets.

SPIELMANN. Yes, the effect on the markets.

CLARA. But will they be affected much?

SPIELMANN. But of course, my dear.

CLARA. Then we may lose all our money.

SPIELMANN. I shouldn't worry about that. These things work themselves out, you know.

CLARA. Everything is going to be different.

SPIELMANN. You are feeling a little nervy tonight. I will turn this thing off. It is tiring you.

CLARA. I have felt it all day. Things are going to be different.

SPIELMANN. In some respects, undoubtedly. But your life will not be affected, my dear. Now the man *I* am sorry for is my poor brother.

CLARA. Oh, the Minister for Public Health.

SPIELMANN. Nothing of the sort. The Minister for Peace.

CLARA. Peace.

SPIELMANN. He's worked to death, poor man. Twenty-four hours a day at the War Office or Downing Street.

CLARA. Is he like you, doctor?

SPIELMANN. Fairly like. It's only to be expected. He's my twin, you know.

CLARA. I should love to meet him.

SPIELMANN. That can be easily arranged.

CLARA. Wasn't it he . . .

SPIELMANN. In fact, we might ask him here this evening. I could ring him up and ask him to come round.

CLARA. But you say he is so busy?

SPIELMANN. He won't be when he resigns.

CLARA. You mean we have to wait for him till he resigns?

SPIELMANN. That will happen any minute now. He's Minister for Peace. The Minister for Peace automatically resigns on the declaration of war.

CLARA. How terrible.

SPIELMANN. But next day they make him minister for something else.

CLARA. Is he a very peaceful man?

SPIELMANN. In a manner of speaking, yes. In a manner of speaking, no. He's a fighter. We are all fighters in our family. The pacifists don't like him.

CLARA. They don't like him. How strange!

SPIELMANN. He said the nation must have more battleships. The pacifists didn't see that more battleships were necessary. But they were, of course.

CLARA. Of course. Why were they necessary?

SPIELMANN. To ensure peace, my dear.

CLARA. But now . . .

SPIELMANN. I know what you are going to say. Well, shall I ring him up? I'll ask him to come round for a drink. [*Rings up.*] Hullo. . . . Is that the War Office? . . . etc.

CLARA. A man of action. . . . A strong man
The opposite lead so often,
But in private life they all had their private lives.
How good to meet a figure who was always public,
His hand on the helm for ever.

SPIELMANN. Yes, he will be delighted to come round as soon as he resigns.

CLARA. Is your brother married?

SPIELMANN. Yes, my dear. Happily married.

CLARA. Happily?

SPIELMANN. Yes.

CLARA. That doesn't fit in.

[MOLL *and* PORTRIGHT *appear on the landing outside and listen at the door.*]

SPIELMANN. My brother is a very interesting man. He and I went to the same school. We were always neck and neck. But we chose different professions. Different yet in a way the same. The peace of the community and the peace of the individual.

CLARA. A man who gives all to an idea.

SPIELMANN. Which of us is that, my dear?

[MOLL *and* PORTRIGHT *shake their heads and retire.*]

90

CLARA. You know, doctor, I should like to give my name to something. To have a liner called after me—

Where in the engine-room

The great cranks plod with their Assyrian feet

Saying Clara de Groot, Clara de Groot, Clara de Groot—

[*The telephone rings.*]

You answer it, doctor. It frightens me.

SPIELMANN. Hullo. Yes. [*To* CLARA.] It's all right, it's for me. Yes, Dr. Spielmann speaking. Yes. I'll go straight down to Downing Street. [*Rings off.*]

I am very, very sorry, my dear. I must leave you immediately.

CLARA. What has happened?

SPIELMANN. The Prime Minister has gone mad.

CLARA. Oh what a terrible thing.

SPIELMANN. I was expecting it. He was an old patient of mine. The crisis has been too much for him.

Well, my dear, I'll see you tomorrow at three. If my brother comes, please give him my apologies. Good-bye. [*Exit.*]

CLARA. Oh God!

Lost my cue and an evening to spend by myself

With not a single engagement.

Such a thing has never happened before.

[*She turns on the radio. Light music.* CLARA *moves round the room nervously in time to the music and stops in front of the picture of Venus, which is covered.*]

91

I *must* look once at this picture. [*Is about to raise the cover when the radio interrupts.*]

RADIO VOICE. The programme of dance music from the Tower of Babel Hotel is being interrupted for an important announcement. Ten minutes ago Parliament was dissolved immediately following upon the declaration of war by His Majesty's government in answer to— [CLARA *hurriedly turns it off.*]

CLARA. War!

That will mean Dr. Spielmann's brother.

He will be coming to see me.

The Great Man, the Minister of Peace.

Supposing he should be like my dream of the Great Man.

    [*She leans back and closes her eyes. A Viennese Waltz is played. The dream-figure of* SIR SHOLTO SPIELMANN *appears in a purple aura in evening dress, white tie and decorations.*]

CLARA [*with her eyes closed*]. It is you.

SIR SHOLTO S. It is I.

CLARA. My dream!

SIR SHOLTO S. [*holding out his white-gloved hands dramatically.*] You see these hands—

Scarred with carrying the cross of my native land

Now to no purpose.

I saw the trouble coming, I gave the warning.

Without any thought of self I gave each pulse of the heart,

Each cell of the brain, each second of each minute of my life

92

To the sacred cause of the propagation of peace.
I have fought the good fight and lost.
Nothing can now console me for my defeat.

CLARA. My love! My dream! My love! [*With her eyes still shut she opens her arms to him. He sinks on his knees and lays his head in her lap.*]

SIR SHOLTO S. Clara! My consolation! [*Blackout. When the lights go on again* CLARA *is alone on the sofa.* MOLL *and* PORTRIGHT *are again on the landing.* CLARA *opens her eyes and stares.*]

CLARA. He is gone.

I am so tired. I must lie down. [*Goes into her bedroom and lies on the bed.*]

MOLL. She has gone, I think.

PORTRIGHT. Are you sure?

MOLL. I will try the key. [*She opens the door and they enter slowly on tiptoe.*]

PORTRIGHT. Ah, there! There! My picture!

MOLL [*in a whisper*]. Quiet, darling.

[*Looking round the room.*] God, what taste!

PORTRIGHT [*going up and standing in front of the picture*]. Return of the goddess after the long separation. . . .

MOLL. Hurry, darling, you can't make your speeches here. Do your little bit of burglary.

PORTRIGHT. It isn't burglary.

[*Next door* CLARA *sits up on her bed and turns the light on.*]

CLARA. I can't rest. [*She gets up.*]

MOLL. Quick. She's coming. [PORTRIGHT *grabs at the*

93

picture and cannot move it.] There's no time. Take cover somewhere. [MOLL *gets into the cupboard.* PORTRIGHT *goes behind the screen.* CLARA *enters from bedroom.*]

CLARA. My nerves are terrible.

                               [*She goes up to the picture.*]

Let me look at this thing.

                               [*She lets up the cover.*]

It seems to me to look rather like me.

[She turns away and walks up and down the room.]

But all day long I've been seeing my face in the
    air—

My own face all the time.

A lovely face but it oughtn't to be in the air.

How dare they turn on this War?

And where's Jenny got to? I can't dress without
    Jenny.

Clara would look nice dressed up tonight.

Why is that door ajar? Everything is on edge to-
    night.

                        [*She locks* MOLL'S *cupboard.*]

Well, if Jenny's not here, I shall just go out as I am.

I must change my shoes.

[She goes back into her bedroom and looks absently for her shoes. Meanwhile PORTRIGHT *comes out from behind the curtain.*]

PORTRIGHT [*looking at the picture*]. Good God! It's changed.

It didn't look like that before.

Look at its eyes, my God, look at its eyes.

94

CLARA [*while putting on her shoes, in a different voice, as if under hypnosis*]. Some one said that shoes had personality,

That when you die your shoes. . . .
That the frozen overflow of personality
Hangs on in jags after the general thaw
When a man has died.
Icicles, acroteria.
In a corner, in a cloakroom, among rackets and rods
An old pair of brogues
With criss-cross wrinkles like an old man's face.
Or when a girl has died
Her shoes are lined up, spruce as soldiers,
Waiting for the word Dismiss.
And in hotels at night passing from door to door
There is something terrible in all those empty shoes.
Frozen overflow of personality . . .
But Clara's got all my personality.

PORTRIGHT. I don't like that picture. I want somebody else.

[CLARA *re-enters the sitting-room.*]

CLARA [*screams*]. Who are you? [*No answer.*]
Have you come for my jewels? [*No answer.*]
Is it blackmail? [*No answer.*]
Are you a reporter? [*No answer.*]
What are you?

PORTRIGHT. I am a painter.

CLARA. A what?

PORTRIGHT. A painter.

CLARA. What have you come to paint?

PORTRIGHT. Nothing.

CLARA. Nothing?

PORTRIGHT. I have painted it already. There it is.

CLARA. Did you paint that?

PORTRIGHT. Yes.

CLARA. How did you come to make it like me?

PORTRIGHT. Did I? [*He looks at it carefully.*]
I had a model. She wasn't you.

CLARA. But it *is* like me, isn't it?

PORTRIGHT. Yes, it is. It seems to have changed. [*He now looks at* CLARA.] But it is not worthy of you.

CLARA. Who said it was?

PORTRIGHT. And another thing. Its eyes are different.
Your eyes are China blue, beautiful, expressionless,
But *those* eyes, look at them. . . .

CLARA. Cover it up.

PORTRIGHT [*covering it*]. Cover her face; mine eyes dazzle; she never died.
Pictures ought to be dead, don't you think?

CLARA. Won't you take it away?

PORTRIGHT. No. I don't want it any more.

CLARA. Then you must go yourself.

PORTRIGHT. I won't go.

CLARA. You can't stay here. I'm going, anyway.

PORTRIGHT. Then let me come with you.

CLARA. Where to?

PORTRIGHT. Wherever you're going.

CLARA. I don't know where I'm going.

PORTRIGHT. Who does?

CLARA. I have an idea.

Have you ever seen Clara de Groot on the pictures?

PORTRIGHT. But you're Clara de Groot.

CLARA. Yes, but have you seen her on the pictures?

PORTRIGHT. Of course I have.

CLARA. Then let's go and see her again. It will do me good. I'm not myself tonight.

PORTRIGHT. But she's yourself.

CLARA. Yes, she is. But what about the crowds in the streets?

PORTRIGHT. What crowds?

CLARA. There were such crowds when I came in. Waiting for the war.

PORTRIGHT. But the war has come. It is here.

CLARA. Then they will be still worse. They will be riotous.

PORTRIGHT. Why should they be? A war has been declared. Well, what of it? It's nothing to make a song and dance about. You don't have to go to it. Nor shall I.

CLARA. But if it comes to us?

PORTRIGHT. It won't, my beloved. Not now. Not now we have found each other.

CLARA. They will conscript you.

PORTRIGHT. Oh no they won't. I shall conscientiously object.

CLARA. Well then they will shoot you.

PORTRIGHT. Let them try. Come, Clara, let us go and see you on the pictures. And don't think about the war. It won't affect us, I tell you. It's nothing to

make a song and dance about. [*They go out. Silence.*
MOLL *beats on the door of the cupboard.*]
MOLL. Let me out of here. Let me out.

Portright. Where have you gone to?

[*A masked couple enter and dance. The* RADIO-
ANNOUNCER, *in evening dress, stands beside
them and sings in a whisper.*]

ANNOUNCER'S SONG

We're out of the picture,
    Out of the picture.
Once we made a song and dance
Every man his own free lance
Every girl a Circe or
A Helen on a golden floor,
Once we held the pose—and how!
    But now
We're out of the picture,
    Out of the picture now.

We're out of the picture,
    Out of the picture.
No more we comb our auburn locks
Among the Quattrocento rocks
And stand as harlequin no more
Upon the grey nostalgic shore,
Once we graced a galleon's prow
    But now
We're out of the picture,
    Out of the picture now.

98

We're out of the picture,
    Out of the picture.
Not free to wear the bishop's gown,
The hero's belt, the martyr's crown,
Not rich enough to keep the tone
Nor call our bloody souls our own,
No private niche these times allow
    For now
We're out of the picture,
    Out of the picture now.

We're out of the picture,
   · Out of the picture.
The foreground needs men in the mass
Beneath a sky of bombs and gas;
The daily grind, the common street
Dethrone, disown the old élite.
Our carriage founders in the slough
    For now
We're out of the picture,
    Out of the picture now.

                    [Then all three move out silently.]

MOLL [*from the cupboard*]. Let me out.

    [SIR SHOLTO SPIELMANN *appears on the land-ing and knocks once or twice. Then noticing that the door is ajar he enters the sitting-room. He is very like his brother but looks several years older and more human. He wears a dinner jacket.*]

SIR SHOLTO S. A, h'm!

MOLL. Let me out.

SIR SHOLTO S. What's that?

MOLL. Let me out of here. I'm in the cupboard.

> [SIR SHOLTO SPIELMANN *unlocks the cupboard and* MOLL *steps out.*]

SIR SHOLTO S. You are Miss de Groot?

MOLL [*after a moment's hesitation*]. Yes.

SIR SHOLTO S. I am Sir Sholto Spielmann.

MOLL. How do you do? Tricky thing that cupboard. It locks automatically.

SIR SHOLTO S. Does this often happen to you?

MOLL. Oh quite often, Sir Sholto. I'm so careless. It's the artistic temperament.

SIR SHOLTO S. Quite so. My brother—

MOLL. He's gone down to Downing Street.

SIR SHOLTO S. The Prime Minister, I suppose? [MOLL *nods.*]

> Well, we all knew it was coming.

MOLL. May I offer you a drink, Sir Sholto?

SIR SHOLTO S. Thank you, Miss de Groot, but I don't know that I really should stay now—

MOLL. Oh yes, you must stay. You look tired.

SIR SHOLTO S. I certainly am. I have just resigned from the Ministry.

MOLL. Then you must be tired. [*She pours him a drink.*] I have never had to resign from anything but I can imagine what it feels like.

SIR SHOLTO S. Oh I am quite pleased, you know. I want to retire and live with my wife and family.

MOLL. But won't they offer you something else?

Sir Sholto S. Certainly they will but I won't take it. I have had enough of public life. My eldest is fifteen, he is a boy, and my youngest is three.

Moll. And he is a boy too?

Sir Sholto S. No, he is a girl. We have a place in the New Forest.

Moll. Sir Sholto, may I talk shop for a moment. The war—

Sir Sholto S. At this time of year it is charming. My children all take riding lessons.

Moll. This war, Sir Sholto—

Sir Sholto S. My wife is having a new greenhouse built—

Moll [*shouting*]. This war, Sir Sholto!

Sir Sholto S. I'm sorry. This war, did you say? What about this war?

Moll. That's what I'm asking you.

Sir Sholto S. My dear Miss de Groot, I have retired from public life. I know nothing further about wars.

Moll. But you *must know*, Sir Sholto. You *must* know if this war is going to be like the last one. Or will it all peter out to nothing?

Sir Sholto S. I would rather talk about something else.

Moll. Tell me at least this. Will there be general conscription?

Sir Sholto S. Tomorrow probably.

Moll. So that's that.

Sir Sholto S. I often envy my brother. We went to

school together. We were always neck and neck. He chose the service of the individual; I chose the service of the State. I often regret my choice.

MOLL. Someone has to serve the State.

SIR SHOLTO S. Someone has to be the Public Hangman. Do you see this attaché-case? It contains the latest lethal weapons for the pocket or handbag. These were produced today for ratification by the War Office and my colleagues kindly bestowed the samples on me as a parting gift. My eldest son will like to have them.

MOLL. May I see them?

SIR SHOLTO S. Certainly. [*Opens the case and takes out several sheaves of typescript, which he lays on the table.*]

MOLL. Is that your lethal weapon?

SIR SHOLTO S. [*laughs*]. In a manner of speaking, yes. No, Miss de Groot, this is what I mean. [*Takes out a revolver and lays it on the table.* MOLL *stretches out her hand to take it but he restrains her.*] Don't touch it. It's still loaded. My colleagues were having a little practice with it.

MOLL. Is that what you do at the War Office?

SIR SHOLTO S. Relaxation, you know. It is an interesting weapon. The inventor is a Swede. But here we have something quite diabolical. [*He produces a bottle of small white tablets.*] You see? They look like aspirin. But are they aspirin, Miss de Groot? No.

MOLL. Poison, I suppose?

SIR SHOLTO S. One of the safest poisons yet invented. Painless and cannot be traced. The patient will be

102

dead within two hours from taking his dose. He will not even notice it.

MOLL. But you are not going to show that to your son?

SIR SHOLTO S. No, I shall keep that for my dogs. I am very fond of dogs, I have six. I don't think any dog should be allowed to live beyond the age of ten. It tires them.

MOLL. You are a very kind man, Sir Sholto.

SIR SHOLTO S. Do you mean that, Miss de Groot? No doubt you think that because I show you a revolver—

MOLL. You are really a gory militarist? No, no, Sir Sholto, I think it is just the boy in you.

SIR SHOLTO S. Thank you. You are quite right. I find these things fascinating as toys. But war is another matter.

MOLL. And your battleships? Were they toys too?

SIR SHOLTO S. No. They were a safeguard of peace. But fascinating also in their way. I am very fond of mechanical things. Down in our place in the New Forest we are thinking of installing one of these new electrical incubators—

MOLL. Forgive me, Sir Sholto, if I seem to be inquisitive. Inquisitive and perhaps hypercritical. You were Minister for Peace and you precipitated the country into war—

SIR SHOLTO S. Precipitated!

MOLL. Yes, precipitated. And what happens now? The country goes to war and you go to the New Forest.

SIR SHOLTO S. I am an old man, Miss de Groot.

MOLL. That's lucky for you, Sir Sholto.

SIR SHOLTO S. You are a little bitter, aren't you?

MOLL. More than a little, Sir Sholto. But not on principle. I am not a pacifist nor a communist nor a propagandist nor an ameliorist.

SIR SHOLTO S. Just a woman in love.

MOLL. How clever of you, Sir Sholto. You ought to have been your brother.

SIR SHOLTO S. And my brother ought to have been me. Public life, people in the masses, those are beyond me. I like people as individuals.

MOLL. I congratulate you. I also condole with you.

SIR SHOLTO S. Well, my dear, tell me about your young man.

MOLL. He is an artist.

SIR SHOLTO S. In that case no doubt he is an introvert—frustrated, overanxious, unproductive.

MOLL. He is all those things.

SIR SHOLTO S. Well, it's not his fault, poor chap. This isn't a world for art.

MOLL. And what about you with your machines and incubators? Isn't that your little art-hobby?

SIR SHOLTO S. Oh my incubator!

MOLL. Have another drink.

SIR SHOLTO S. Thank you.

MOLL. And what about the housewife dusting the mantelpiece? And the golfer perfecting his swing in the pierglass? Are they all doomed because they are amateur artists, martyrs to their hankering for perfection?

SIR SHOLTO S. I don't know.

MOLL. So you like people as individuals?

And you say this is no world for the artist.

Perhaps it is no world for the individual?

SIR SHOLTO S. I am tired and old with work I did not ask for,

I should have done better in some other line.

MOLL. Perhaps you would like to lie down?

SIR SHOLTO S. I am more tired than I thought. For-give me, Miss de Groot, but I *should* like to lie down.

MOLL. Of course, Sir Sholto. Will you come in here?

[*She leads* SIR SHOLTO, *who is tottering with fatigue, into the bedroom. He takes off his shoes and coat and lies on the bed.* MOLL *returns to the sitting-room and studies the picture.*]

MOLL. What did he want to paint it for anyway?

Crucifying himself, living in a fool's purgatory.

Though I must admit there is something about the eyes.

[PORTRIGHT *bursts in from the landing door, running.*]

PORTRIGHT. Hullo!

MOLL. Hullo! Where's your lady?

PORTRIGHT. Waiting for me. Waiting. Where did she say it was?

MOLL. What was?

PORTRIGHT. Don't fuss me. Where was it she said? The right-hand corner of something.

MOLL. Feckless as ever!

[PORTRIGHT *rummages in the cupboard and produces a string of coloured beads.*]

PORTRIGHT. Here it is.

MOLL [*stopping him as he hurries to the door*]. Not so fast, my dear. Does it occur to you that you came to this room with me? And that you left me locked up in a cupboard and walked off with somebody else? What is that thing?

PORTRIGHT. It's for her nerves.

MOLL. Oh yes?

PORTRIGHT. She holds it in her fingers and slips the beads along—tells them, you know—and then everything seems all right.

MOLL. That's nice, isn't it?

PORTRIGHT. I must go now, Moll.

MOLL. And what about me?

PORTRIGHT. Oh that's all right, Moll. I don't want the picture any more, I've changed my mind.

MOLL. I see. You've changed your mind and I've served my turn.

PORTRIGHT. What's wrong with you, Moll?

MOLL. What's wrong with you, you fool? Give me that thing. [*She snatches the beads from him.*]

PORTRIGHT. Damn you, Moll. Give it back, Clara's waiting.

MOLL. Oh, Clara's waiting?
    Do you know there's a war on?

PORTRIGHT. Yes. What about it?

MOLL. Tomorrow there will be conscription for all. All includes you.

106

PORTRIGHT. No, it doesn't.

[MOLL *turns on the radio.*]

RADIO. All able-bodied male persons between the ages of sixteen and sixty must give in their names before noon tomorrow to their regional recruiting officers. Anyone omitting to do this will be liable to immediate imprisonment with hard labour— [MOLL *turns it off.*]

MOLL. There you are.

PORTRIGHT. Damn.

MOLL. So it's good-bye Clara.

PORTRIGHT. Not yet. I've got till noon tomorrow.

MOLL. You won't get far with Clara in that time. Didn't you know? She's the Diana of the films.

[PORTRIGHT *sits down by the table. Suddenly he notices the revolver and picks it up.*]

PORTRIGHT. What's this?

MOLL. What do you think?

PORTRIGHT. I've never had one in my hand before. Only in dreams.

MOLL. Very Freudian of you.

PORTRIGHT. I often have them in dreams. And I always hit.

MOLL. You wouldn't find that in real life.

PORTRIGHT. How do you aim, Moll?

MOLL. Like this, darling. [*She takes the revolver and cocks it.*] Hold it like this by your side. Then raise it slowly with your arm practically straight. Keep raising it, don't check at all, and fire while your arm is still lifting before the sight covers the target.

Don't try to hold it steady and aim. Revolver shooting is snap-shooting.

PORTRIGHT. Why don't you fire?

MOLL. Nothing to fire at, ducky.

PORTRIGHT. That's just it. If only there was!

MOLL. Feeling vicious?

PORTRIGHT. It's because I'm always frustrated. I take such trouble and what do I get for it?

MOLL. You don't take any trouble.

PORTRIGHT. I produce a masterpiece and it is stolen. I meet the woman of my dreams and the country goes and conscripts me.

MOLL. Never mind. It'll give you something to fire at.

PORTRIGHT. No. That won't do. [*Takes up the revolver and weighs it in his hand.*] I should like to use this on an enemy. Not on a vague enemy fifty yards away in a trench but on someone who is really responsible—on one of the brutes who drive us against the wall. I can see it all, you know. I'm not such a fool as you think I am. A fool certainly but not such a fool as you think I am. You think I'm an utter egotist, that all the war means to me is something that comes between me and Clara. Well that *is* what chiefly concerns me. Why lie about it?

MOLL. Yes, why lie about it? The war comes between you and Clara and it comes between me and you. The latter case seems to me the more important.

PORTRIGHT. How do you mean me and you?

MOLL. Oh I dare say it was just that psycho-analyst and his blague about your picture. I must be ex-

tremely suggestible. However, suggestible or not, I
like you far more than you like Clara.

PORTRIGHT. But I don't like Clara. I love her.

MOLL. Oh yes?

PORTRIGHT. I have never really loved outside my art.
And when I meet it the war steps in—

MOLL [*sings*]. I once had a dear little doll, dears—

PORTRIGHT. Are you laughing at me?

MOLL. Yes, darling. If you want to shoot someone, you
had better shoot me.

PORTRIGHT. No, not you, darling.

MOLL. Thank you for that kind word. [*Kisses him.*]

PORTRIGHT [*surprised*]. What kind word?

MOLL. You called me darling.

PORTRIGHT. Oh, did I?

MOLL. Ah, you little beast!

PORTRIGHT. You know, I feel stronger than I did.
Something has entered into me.

MOLL. But not strong enough?

PORTRIGHT. No. The world is too much with us—grab
and snatch on the one side and stuffed dummies on
the other. Some day I'll blow the stuffing out of
them—the half-baked masters who damn us with
good intentions. If I could meet one of them!
[*Poises the revolver.*]
   And if I could only escape,
   Escape the pastiche of other people's dreams
   And feel the handle of an axe grow in my hand
   And feel the axe draw up the arm to strike!
   But the Old Guard are too strong for us,

109

Our uniformed fears and instincts, our conven-
tions

Always ready to deploy on every landscape,

Preclude all shelter in the wanton woods.

Nous n'irons plus au bois.

MOLL. Don't be so tragic, darling. You're posing.

PORTRIGHT. Who wouldn't be? One may as well go
down with a gesture.

I'll kill one of them. I will. I will.

[*A spruce* YOUNG MAN *appears on the landing
and knocks at the door.*]

MOLL. Come in.

YOUNG MAN [*entering*]. Excuse me. I am Sir Sholto
Spielmann's secretary. They told me I should find
him here.

MOLL. Yes. Sir Sholto is here.

PORTRIGHT [*to* MOLL]. What are you talking about?

[*To* YOUNG MAN.] Who the devil are you? [*He
waves the revolver at him.*]

MOLL. Put that down, darling.

YOUNG MAN. Could I see Sir Sholto?

PORTRIGHT. Sir Sholto hell! There's no Sir Sholto here.

MOLL. How unlike yourself you're becoming.

PORTRIGHT [*pleased*]. I am, aren't I? Oh yes, there are
going to be damn alterations round here. I'm on
top in this little room. I've got the armaments.

MOLL [*to* YOUNG MAN]. It's all right. It's only his
fun.

YOUNG MAN. Well, could I see Sir Sholto? It's urgent.

PORTRIGHT. If Sir Sholto's here, I'll shoot him.

110

MOLL [*grabs at revolver*]. Stop fooling, darling.

> [SIR SHOLTO *appears in the doorway of the bed-room, without his coat and in his socks. He is still dropping with sleep.*]

SIR SHOLTO S. Did someone call me?

PORTRIGHT [*shouting*]. Are you Sir Sholto Spielmann?

SIR SHOLTO S. Yes, young man. What are you doing with that gun?

PORTRIGHT. What does anyone do with guns?

SIR SHOLTO S. Oh hullo, Edwards. What is it?

YOUNG MAN. You must come at once, sir.

PORTRIGHT. Shut up, you. May I ask you something, Sir Sholto?

SIR SHOLTO S. Yes.

PORTRIGHT. Are you the man who made us have more battleships?

SIR SHOLTO S. I am.

PORTRIGHT. The Minister for Peace?

SIR SHOLTO S. I was Minister of Peace but I have re-signed. I am retiring from public life.

PORTRIGHT. It was time you did. Now I am going to shoot you.

SIR SHOLTO S. Don't be silly, young man.

PORTRIGHT. Silly! [*He shoots and* SIR SHOLTO *falls.*]

YOUNG MAN. Help, help!

MOLL [*examining* SIR S.]. Well, you hit that time any-way.

PORTRIGHT. Is he dead? [MOLL *nods.*] Good.

YOUNG MAN. Oh my God. [*He runs out.*]

MOLL. Stop! There, he's gone.

PORTRIGHT. And now for Clara. [*He throws the revolver down with a gesture.*]

MOLL. No more Clara now, darling.

PORTRIGHT. Oh, conscription?

MOLL. No, darling, the dock. They will come and arrest you for murder.

PORTRIGHT. Never mind. It was worth it. But I will see Clara before that.

MOLL. Why not see me? A bird in the hand, you know.

PORTRIGHT. But I don't love you, Moll.

MOLL. What is love? Merely a matter of suggestion.

PORTRIGHT. It's not. Love is something predestined.

MOLL. I could make you forget Clara in five minutes.

PORTRIGHT. No, you couldn't.

MOLL. Shall we try?

PORTRIGHT. No, I must go. Clara is waiting for her beads.

MOLL [*picking up the beads from the table*]. She can wait a little longer. Give me five minutes and you're welcome to Clara if I fail.

PORTRIGHT. All right.

[MOLL *goes into the bedroom and begins to look through* CLARA'S *wardrobe.*]

PORTRIGHT. I was wrong in trying to make my love from paint;

These things cannot be forced. We find them like the wind

Which springs abruptly from a quiet sea.

I did not know what I wanted,

But all I wanted was another human being.

112

MOLL [*from bedroom*]. Not even a human being, darling. What fetched you—we'll prove it in a moment.

[*The lights go out.*]

MOLL. Damn! What's happened now?

[*Picks up the bedroom telephone.*]

Hullo! Hullo! That the operator? What's happened to the lights? Oh my God! Thank you. [*Rings off.*]

PORTRIGHT. What is it, Moll?

Why have the lights gone out?

MOLL [*from bedroom*]. The lights have gone out because there is going to be an air-raid.

PORTRIGHT. Oh. But what about Clara?

MOLL. Just give me my five minutes.

PORTRIGHT. Then for God's sake let's have some music. [*Turns on* RADIO.]

RADIO. . . . and that is all that now remains of Paris. The destruction was completed under schedule time. The remaining population is calculated at not more than—

[PORTRIGHT *turns it off to jazz.* MOLL *appears carrying two candles and dressed in a most sumptuous négligé belonging to* CLARA.]

PORTRIGHT. Clara!

MOLL. I'm not Clara.

PORTRIGHT. Who are you then? [*He sinks on his knees before her.*]

MOLL. *Quod erat demonstrandum.*

I am afraid you were always one for the surface.

Never mind, darling, I am not going to scold you.

There is not time for that.
If you like these furbelows it's all that matters;
I'm inside them. Do you want me?

PORTRIGHT. Please, Moll, please.

MOLL. Then let us have a drink on it. [*She pours out two glasses. Into* PORTRIGHT'S *she puts a white tablet from* SIR SHOLTO'S *bottle.*]

MOLL. Prosit.

PORTRIGHT. Prosit.

> [*The radio jazz fades out in violent atmospherics.* MOLL *points to the bedroom door and* PORTRIGHT *goes through it.* MOLL, *remaining, stands for a moment in front of the picture.*]

MOLL. Venus . . . a non-existent goddess!

> [*She turns and stands with her back to the picture.*]

He will be dead in two hours.
He does not know it.
I poisoned him.
A painless death.
I poisoned him to save him,
To save him from prison and, if not prison, from war
And if not war from life.
For what would remain for him?
Tonight he has confidence but it would not last.
And tonight he will have love—my love—
But that would not last either.

> [*She moves towards the bedroom door, stops again and sings.*]

I gave him poison,
   He drank it down,
He will be dead
   In two hours' time
But worse things happen in this town.

He could not live,
   I cannot die
He will be dead
   In two hours' time
And I will face the lonely sky.

He will have lived
   Before he sink,
He will have lived
   Two hours of time,
And that is more than you may think.

               [*She enters the bedroom.*]
[*The picture of* VENUS *on the wall is suddenly rent and* VENUS *steps out of it. She looks very different from the* VENUS *of the picture. She walks up to the partition wall and rolls it round so that it lies diagonally, cutting off the bedroom in the left corner of the* STAGE. VENUS *stands in midstage and addresses the audience.*]

VENUS. So you think it is all a matter of love?
And what do you think love is a matter of?
Matter is the word for it.
Atoms—permutations, combinations of atoms.
It's not just a fancy ballet, a *fête champêtre*.

115

The cycle of life demands to be repeated.
You were made by your parents, you must make in
    return,
You must make children for Death.
Death is a sculptor, you must quarry him marble,
His chisel will find the shape in the blind block.
What you call love is merely an incident;
Wait till you see the end of it.
There is a city beyond this life, no flesh or blood
    there,
No food in the shops, no fire in the grates, no smoke
    from the chimneys;
All the people that have ever lived walk there
Renouncing their living,
All the people that have ever loved walk there
Renouncing their loving,
But they do not even think this renunciation
For their brains are solid, of stone,
Their heads and their eyes are of stone,
Being no longer organisms of nature
But final versions of an artist's vision.
For the art of man is supererogation;
Man himself will be a work of art in the end.
Man should not emulate the artist, Death.
Let not man be contriving a frozen beauty;
While he is here and now let him deal in here and
    now,
Work and fight for meat and love,
Gallant approximation, bravado of defeat.
I am the principle of Unity and Division,

116

Multiplication by pain,
Spawning of worlds from a discord
Always recurring,
I am the attempt to cover the abyss with grass
And to spangle the grass with flowers
And to put there cattle grazing the grass
And young men picking the flowers,
And to make believe through elaboration of pattern
That life goes on for ever.
Which, thanks to me, is true in a sense.
Which, thanks to me, is true in the world of sense
Though it is not true in the world of precise death,
The world of pure idea, mating statues.
Go to your work, children, the tide is coming in,
The strip of sand is narrow,
You have not much time if you wish to get married,
You have not much time if you wish to build castles.
Blessed are the reckless spendthrifts of vitality
But blessed also are all who last the course,
Blessed are those who endure as a point of etiquette
And blessed are the cynics who carry their cross as a
        gesture.
Do you remember when you were six years old
The text in the parish church at Christmas,
'Peace on Earth, Goodwill to Men',
And Christ's lips moving in the stained glass win-
        dow.
There were no lipreaders present
But I can tell you what he said.
'I come bringing not peace,' he said. 'I come

117

Bringing not peace but a sword.'
All to their posts. The drum is beating.
Diver, descend. Ploughman, drive your team.
Grapple the bulk of the sea, challenge the flinty
    soil;
The furrows are there in advance as music is there
    in the air
Waiting to be realised upon the fiddler's bow.

                            [VENUS *goes out.*]

BOTH. For two hours you and I together, then we depart.

CHORUS [*off*]. Sleep and wake, sleep and wake,
               Sleep to wake but wake to sleep,
               And body calling body make
               A further body, the insistent task
               Of rolling a stone up the steep
               Hill of hell, of rolling a stone
               Away from the tomb and do not ask
               Who comes forth in the dawn alone.

            CURTAIN

ACT II

SCENE II

[*The same. Noise and lights of an air-raid. Except for these flashes of light the stage is dark. The flashes show the gaping picture of* Venus *with a solid wall behind it. Someone is heard stumbling upstairs and* Clara *appears dishevelled and panic-stricken on the landing.*]

Clara. The end of the world!

> [*She unlocks the door and enters sitting-room.*]

I must get to bed, I must cover my head with the clothes.

But where is the door to my bedroom?

Where has the wall gone? Where is the door?

Nothing is where it was.

The door ought to be here. I can't find it.

Perhaps I have forgotten.

It is Clara. She can't remember.

> [*She sinks down on the floor.*]

Clara can't remember.

Voices [*off*]. She will remember less when she is dead.

Clara. Who's that?

> [*A shell falls outside.*]

Or if only I could get into bed.

If only I could remember where the door is.

VOICE [*off*]. When we are dead what shall we remember?

ANSWERING CHORUS. Shall we remember the jingles
>   of the morning,
The pipers the pedlars and the brass farthings,
The buds of music, the imagined darlings?
>   No, we shall *not* remember.

Shall we remember the games with puffball and
>   plaintain,
Searching for the lost handle to the silent fountain,
Hiding in the shrubbery, shutting our eyes and
>   counting?

Shall we remember the marigolds parading,
Smell of grass and noise of the corncrake railing
And the fun of dragging a stick along the paling?

And after that shall we remember the races,
The broken tape, the clamour of companions'
>   voices,
The schoolboy's callow joys in smut and curses?

And shall we remember our early adult pleasure,
The dive in love's lagoons of brilliant azure,
The gay martyrdom, the brave fantasia.

Shall we remember the kick of inspired religion,
The visions in drink, the feel of the homing pigeon
Drawn by a magnet to an intuited region?

Shall we remember the noise of the moving nations
Or shall we remember the gusty sun's creations,
The night and the never-to-be-climbed-to constel-
lations?
No, we shall *not* remember.

[CLARA *suddenly screams. She has found the
body of* SIR SHOLTO. *She begins to look round
and finds a matchbox. She strikes several matches
in her nervousness before she can see who he is.*]

CLARA. Sir Sholto Spielmann!
The only great man I have ever met!
And I only met him in a dream.

[*Enter* MOLL, *still in* CLARA's *clothes, with a
candle in her hand.*]

CLARA. Who are you?

MOLL. Who are you?

CLARA. I am Clara de Groot. Clara de Groot the actress.

MOLL. No, you're not. She's gone.

CLARA. Gone where?

MOLL. Gone with the rest of them.

CLARA. This is my flat.

MOLL. Not any longer.

CLARA. Let me in there. You're mad. Let me in to my
bedroom.

MOLL. You can't go in there. There is a dead man in there.

CLARA. But there is a dead man here.

MOLL. There are dead men everywhere, Clara.
Come. Help me to push back this wall.

[MOLL *and* CLARA *push the bedroom wall right
back level with the wings of the stage.*]

121

Now, that is forgotten.
He was a man whom I loved.
He was a failure and he had to die.
Out of that world I am the only residue.
And you, Clara, I do not really know . . .
What am I to do with you, Clara?
You do not really belong here any more.
Your world is in bits already.
With gunnery practice on the downs of chalk
They practised scales against the concert day;
But after they have played and men go home
If any home remains
Then I tell you, if any home remains,
People like me will hold it, people like me
Will hold the world together as if with walls.
And if no home remains but men survive
People like me will build the survivors homes.
As long as we keep the courage of our limbs
Our animal instincts and our human soul—
> [*Knocking on the door. Enter four men in uni-
> form with revolvers.*]

LEADER. Where is the man Portright?
MOLL. What do you want with him.
LEADER. We have been sent to get him.
MOLL. You are too late.
LEADER. Search the place.
> [*The four men search the room methodically and
> find* SIR SHOLTO'S *corpse. They take off their hats
> and stand for a moment with their heads bowed.
> Then they go on with their search mechanically*].

LEADER. Where does that door lead to?

MOLL. It did lead to the bedroom.

> [*The* LEADER *opens it. A blank wall is revealed.*]

LEADER. What is this?

MOLL. That? That is a blank wall. In other words that is the irrevocable moment.

LEADER [*to his men*]. Come here. See if you can break this down.

> [*They batter on the wall.*]

MOLL. You will never see light that way.

> [*They desist.*]

LEADER. Carry out the body.

> [*They carry out the body of* SIR SHOLTO.]
> [MOLL *goes over to the window and pulls back the curtains.*]

MOLL. Clara!

Did you ever play that game where you pluck off the petals of flowers?

One by one, you know—and count—

'He loves me, he loves me not.'

Did you ever play that game?

> [CLARA *nods.*]

Well then, my dear, come over here to the window.

> [CLARA *comes over to her.*]

You and I will sit here quietly and count the shells.

> [*A gauze curtain falls, separating* MOLL *and* CLARA *from the front of the stage, where the* AUCTIONEER *appears dressed as a convict and with a stone-breaking hammer.*]

123

AUCTIONEER. One two three four.
   One two three four.
   Can you turn these stones to bread?
   Any offers for a loaf of bread?
   Any offers for a sinking world?
   One two three four,
   One two three four.
   Any offers, ladies and gentlemen?
   Any offers, comrades?
   Any offers, any offers, for a last look at the peep-
      show,
   A seat in the back of the pit at the last perfor-
      mance?
   Think of the good old times and buy a ticket for
      charity—
   Should auld acquaintance be forgot—
   Think of the humdrum comfort of your cherished
      lives
   Safe in the morning train behind perspiring windows
   And in the evening train crumpling the evening
      paper
   Between the dirty green of soccer-fields and the
      shining
   Suburban cemetery and the smoky trees
   Brimming in twilight with the sparrows' palaver;
   Even then you thought you were dragooned to
      duty,
   To dot and carry one and carry one,
   Carry the cross whose arms stretch out to heaven
   Hung with the vermin of minutes, rat and stoat.

One two three four,
One two three four.
The show is closing; is there not a single offer?
If not for love, from a sense of martyred pride?
Was it not good after all to have once been born
And have said to yourself 'This is nobody else but I
And the world about me is mine and therefore
        good—
My world, my mother and mistress, to be fought,
Gained and regained and moulded to my mind,
Ravished from virgin silence, forced to speak
The answer which I felt but could not frame?'
For that world, living still but at such odds
As no insurance company would take,
Who makes a bid, my friends, who makes a bid?
Who gambles on this bird with the broken wing,
This missing engine, this cracked bell, this heap
Of scuttering ants beneath the great beast's foot?
It is your last chance which is here and now—
The naked legs of children laced with foam,
Waving their spades around a tower of sand—
It is going, going, among the flux of words,
Three thousand years of a wordy civilisation,
Tags and slogans, nursery rhymes and prayers
Resolved at last to a drowning gasp for breath.
Our world is going, going—going for a song,
Going for a next to nothing, a nought, a cipher,
Going for the winning time of last year's athletes,
Going for a wisp of paper, a wraith of power,
A cripple's dream of life as a steeple-jack

Or the odds on driving back the one-way street
That leads to death, going for a moment more,
For a last minute speculation on Why and Who—
Who above all it was whom once we loved,
Whose face we cannot remember but whose hands
We still can feel in the dark like a man in a boat
Dangling his hand in the water flowing and going
Going for ever under collapsing bridges
Going going—going through veils of mist
Through walls of air, through gates of glassy music,
Striated dark and never-guessed-at corners,
And over an edge and down a ramp of light.
One two three four,
One two three four.
GOING GOING GOING GONE

MOLL [*from behind the curtain*].
A recurrent sacrifice is still required,
New lives, bubbles of air, still rise from depths be-
        mired,
Rise to the life divined but not desired.
I will give you sons. Good luck go with them.

                CURTAIN

[*The* RADIO-ANNOUNCER *comes in front of the* CURTAIN.]

RADIO-ANNOUNCER. It is not enough
        To have winning ways,
            The trimmed wick burns clear,
        To follow with an indolent eye
        The flicker-pattern of the days,
            For here ends our hoarded oil.

        The acquisitive arts
        Are not enough,
            The trimmed wick burns clear,
        It is a little and a tired time
        To be making money or love,
            Here ends our hoarded oil.

        A kiss, a cuddle,
        A crossed cheque,
            The trimmed wick burns clear,
        Walk among statues in the dark,
        The odds are you will break your neck—
            Here ends our hoarded oil.